THE UNION BOOKSHELF

A Selected Civil War Bibliography

By
Michael Mullins and Rowena Reed

Broadfoot's Bookmark
Wendell, North Carolina
1982

Library of Congress Catalog Card Number: 82-71852

Preface

Students of the Civil War, collectors of Civil War books and others who may wish to acquire a basic library about the war are confronted with a formidable mass of literature. It has been estimated that close to a half million studies, accounts and compilations have been published. The quality, value, and usefulness of these works is by no means uniform.

Several guides for the formation of a library of Confederate books have been published. Douglas S. Freeman's *South to Posterity: An Introduction to the Writing of Confederate History* (N.Y.: Charles Scribner's Sons, 1939), E. Merton Coulter's *Travels in the Confederate States: A Bibliography* (Norman: University of Oklahoma Press, 1948), Richard Harwell's *The Confederate Hundred: A Bibliophilic Selection of Confederate Books* (Urbana, Illinois: Beta Phi Mu, 1964), and *In Tall Cotton: The 200 Most Important Confederate Books for the Reader, Researcher and Collector* (Austin: Jenkins Publishing Company and Frontier America Corporation, 1978) have become standard reference sources for book collectors and dealers. Other books have been published which contain information useful for establishing a general Civil War libarary; for example, *Civil War Books: A Critical Bibliography* edited by Allan Nevins, James I. Robertson, Jr., and Bell I. Wiley (Baton Rouge: Louisiana State University Press, 1967-69) and *A Basic Civil War Library: A Bibliographical Essay* by Ralph E. Newman and E. B. Long (Springfield: Civil War Centennial Commission of Illinois, 1964).

However, the only published guide to Union books is an unannotated list contained in a series of articles by Ralph Newman in Volume I (Nos. 1, 2, and 3) of the journal *Civil War History*. Bruce Catton's review of John J. Pullen's *The Twentieth Maine* (Philadelphia: J. P. Lippincott, 1957) published in the *New York Times Book Review* (10 November 1957) contains comments on a few Union books.

The present volume is intended as a reference source for those interested in studying or collecting books about the Civil War from the Union perspective. It was prepared without restriction to a round number. Instead the authors have selected what they consider the best books regardless of number. Two hundred forty-six books were chosen, including several superior regimental histories and participant accounts. The total number includes books in the supplemental lists of unit histories and personal reminiscences for which there are no annotations. Items on these lists were grouped together to avoid redundancy in annotations; they are of similarly high quality to those in the main section of the guide.

The following basic research sources were considered too familiar to be included:

Annals of the Civil War, by Principal Participants North and South, Philadelphia: The Times Publishing Company, 1879.

Boatner, Mark M., *The Civil War Dictionary*, New York: David McKay Company, 1959.

Dornbusch, Charles E., *Military Bibliography of the Civil War* (3 volumes), New York: The New York Public Library, 1961-1972.

Dyer, Frederick H., *A Compendium of the War of the Rebellion*, Des Moines: The Dyer Publishing Company, 1908.

Fox, William F., *Regimental Losses in the American Civil War 1861-1865*, Albany: Albany Publishing Company, 1889.

Johnson, Robert W., and Clarence C. Buel, *Battles and Leaders of the Civil War...Being for the most Part Contributions by Union and Confederate Officers* (4 volumes), New York: The Century Company, 1887-1888.

Livermore, Thomas L., *Numbers and Losses in the Civil War in America, 1861-1865*, Boston: Houghton, Mifflin and Company, 1900.

Long, E. B., with Barbara Long, *The Civil War Day by Day*, New York: Doubleday and Company, 1971.

Miller, Francis T., *The Photographic History of the Civil War* (10 volumes), New York: The Review of Reviews Company, 1911.

U. S. Congress, *Report of the Joint Committee on the Conduct of the War,* (6 volumes and supplement), Washington, D. C.: Government Printing Office, 1863, 1865-1866.

U. S. Navy Department, Office of Naval War Records, *Official Records of the Union and Confederate Navies in the War of the Rebellion,* (30 volumes and index), Washington, D. C.: Government Printing Office, 1894-1922.

U. S. War Department, *The War of the Rebellion: A Compilation of the Official Records of the Union and Confederate Armies,* (70 volumes in 128 and index), Washington, D. C.: Government Printing Office, 1880-1901.

This guide is by no means definitive. Although the authors, one a long-time collector of Civil War books and Book Review Editor of the *Civil War Book Exchange,* and the other a professional historian of the Civil War, have some claim to good judgment, it is impossible to avoid the subjectivity involved in making choices. Others may disagree. Nevertheless, it is hoped that this book will stimulate further interest in the Northern side of the war.

Reference Abbreviations

Civil War Books A Critical Bibliography (2 volumes) edited by Allan Nevins, James Robertson and Bell Wiley (Baton Rouge: 1967-1969), an annotated list of the vast majority of Civil War books in print at the time is cited as CWB. *A Basic Civil War Library* by Ralph Newman and E. B. Long (Springfield: 1964) is an unannotated list of Union and Confederate books. It is cited as BCWL. *A Union Book Shelf* by Ralph Newman appeared as three articles in *Civil War History* Volume 1, Numbers 1, 2, and 3 (Iowa City: 1955), consisting of an unannotated listing of books that the author chose as being "...an acceptable list of books relating to Northern participation in the war of the sixties." It has been cited as UBS.

Other sources mentioned in the annotations include the periodicals *Civil War History* (Kent, Ohio) and *Civil War Times Illustrated* (Harrisburg, Pennsylvania), specifically their book review departments; *The Book Review Digest* (New York, New York), published annually since 1905, which contains reviews from dozens of sources like *American Historical Review, The New York Times Book Review, Library Journal;* and an article entitled *Great Retellings of a Great Story* by Bruce Catton in *The New York Times Book Review* (November 10, 1957).

Table of Contents

Part I

Annotated Books

1

Adams, George W.

Doctors in Blue, The Medical History of the Union Army in the Civil War   New York: H. Schuman, 1952

xii, 253 pp., illus., index.

The author has admirably compressed much essential information about a neglected topic into the text concerning administration, ambulances, hospitals, medical affairs and nursing. Avery Craven stated "It will fill a gap in our understanding of the war..." *Book Review Digest,* 1952. Supplemental volumes include *Medical Recollections of the Army of the Potomac* by Jonathan Letterman, M. D. (N. Y.: 1866), William H. Reed's *Hospital Life in the Army of the Potomac* (Boston: 1866), Paul E. Steiner's *Physician-generals in the Civil War: A Study in Nineteenth Mid-century American Medicine* (Springfield: 1966) and *Military Medical and Surgical Essays, Prepared for the United States Sanitary Commission* edited by William A. Hammond (Philadelphia, 1864).

References: CWB I, 3; BCWL, 22; Letterman: CWB I, 121; Reed: CWB I, 150; Steiner: CWB II, 136

2

Ambrose, Stephen E.

Halleck: Lincoln's Chief of Staff. Baton Rouge: Louisiana State University Press, 1962

vi, 226 pp., maps, illus., index.

The only biography of this Union administrator and commander-in-chief, Professor Ambrose's short assessment of Halleck's military career demonstrates that general's significant role in the Federal victory and emphasizes the importance of a unified Northern command for the defeat of the South.

References: CWB II, 36; BCWL, 20.

3

Anderson, Bern

By Sea and By River: The Naval History of the Civil War. New York: Alfred A. Knopf, 1962

303 pp., map, illus., index.

Focusing on the Union Navy's strategic aims and results, the author perceptively analyzes the interrelation between the army and the navy and provides superb descriptions of leading naval personalities, despite some minor inaccuracy of details.

Reprinted in 1977 by Greenwood Press (Westport, Connecticut).

References: CWB I, 218; BCWL, 12.

4

Andrews, J. Cutler

The North Reports the Civil War. Pittsburgh: University of Pittsburgh Press, 1955

x, 813 pp., maps, illus., ports., index.

John Hubbell writes in *Civil War Books:* "The war as newspaper correspondents saw it; a thorough treatment of such subjects as censorship, conflicts between press and officers and exploits of individual reporters." Much material from reporter's letters, diaries and dispatches is printed here for the first time. A supplemental volume, which is also excellent study, is Bernard Weisberger's *Reporters for the Union* (Boston, 1953).

References: CWB II, 120; BCWL, 22; UBS I, 3 p. 305; Weisberger: CWB II, 138; UBS I, 3 p. 308.

5

Barber, Lucius W.

Army Memoirs of Lucius W. Barber, Company 'D', 15th Illinois Volunteer Infantry, May 25, 1861 - September 30, 1865. Chicago: J.M.W. Jones Stationery and Printing Company, 1894

v, 242 pp., front. (port.).

James I. Robertson, in *Civil War Books,* aptly observes that "the author's extensive travels during the war, plus his discursive comments on all that he saw, make this one of the better personal narratives by a Federal soldier."

References: CWB I, 54.

6

Bartlett, Asa W.

History of the Twelfth Regiment New Hampshire Volunteers in the War of the Rebellion. Concord: Ira C. Evans, 1897

x, 752, 87 pp., front. (port.), (illus., ports.).

Not as widely publicized as some other regimental histories, this volume is among the best of the Northern unit histories. The regiment served in the Army of the Potomac.

References: CWB I, 54.

7

Bigelow, John

The Campaign of Chancellorsville. New Haven: Yale University Press, 1910

xvi, 528 pp., maps, index.

Fully documented and superbly written, this classic study of a battle is a model for others.

References: CWB I, 23; BCWL, 11.

REMINISCENCES

OF

GENERAL HERMAN HAUPT

Director, Chief Engineer and General Superintendent of the
Pennsylvania Railroad
Contractor and Chief Engineer for the Hoosac Tunnel
Chief of the Bureau of United States Military Railroads in the
Civil War
Chief Engineer of the Tidewater Pipeline
General Manager of the Richmond & Danville and
Northern Pacific Railroads
President American Air Power Company
Etc   Etc

GIVING

HITHERTO UNPUBLISHED OFFICIAL ORDERS,

PERSONAL NARRATIVES OF IMPORTANT MILITARY
OPERATIONS,

AND

INTERVIEWS WITH PRESIDENT LINCOLN, SECRETARY STANTON, GENERAL-
IN-CHIEF HALLECK, AND WITH GENERALS McDOWELL, Mc-
CLELLAN, MEADE, HANCOCK, BURNSIDE, AND OTHERS
IN COMMAND OF THE ARMIES IN THE FIELD,
AND HIS IMPRESSIONS OF THESE MEN

[WRITTEN BY HIMSELF]

WITH NOTES AND A PERSONAL SKETCH BY
FRANK ABIAL FLOWER

Illustrated from Photographs of Actual Operations in the Field

1901

8

Billings, John D.

The History of the Tenth Massachusetts Battery of Light Artillery in the War of the Rebellion. Boston: Hall and Whiting, 1881

xii, 400 pp., front., plates, ports.

A superior unit history the author relied extensively on his own diary, a comrade's unpublished manuscript, and hundreds of letters for this book. The battery served in the Second and Third corps, Army of the Potomac.

Another edition was published by Arakelvan Press (Boston: 1909).

References: CWB I, 60.

9

Billings, John D.

Hardtack and Coffee. Boston: George M. Smith, 1887

vi, 406 pp., illus., plates, ports., front. (colored plates), index.

An indispensable source for information on the Union soldier, filled with delightfully written anecdotes and personal observations.

A new edition skillfully edited by Richard Harwell was published as a Lakeside classic, Chicago: 1960.

References: CWB I, 59, 60; BCWL, 15.

10

Blumenthal, Henry

A Reappraisal of Franco-American Relations, 1830-1871. Chapel Hill: University of North Carolina Press, 1959

xiv, 255 pp.

A scholarly work containing cogent observations of the war years. Blumenthal's book singles out French neutrality as one of the major accomplishments of Federal foreign policy.

References: CWB I, 247.

11

Campaigns of the Civil War (16 volumes). New York: Charles Scribner's Sons, 1881-1885

maps, each volume is indexed.

Series includes 13 volumes on the army and 3 on the navy. Sometimes included in the set is another volume entitled *Gettysburg to the Rapidan: The Army of the Potomac July 1863 to April 1864* by Andrew A. Humphreys. The Army series is a narration of events by various Union officers, except one by John G. Nicolay which describes all significant Northern movements in great detail. The naval series, written mainly by leading participants, informs the reader about naval objectives, strategy, and tactics. Some of the volumes are better than others but, as a unit, they give an excellent description of the entire war.

The set was reprinted by Thomas Yoseloff in New York, 1963 in 8 volumes.

References: CWB I, 13, 25, 26, 27, 29, 31, 33, 39, 40, 41, 42, 48, 229, 234; BCWL, 11; UBS 1, 1 pp. 72.

12
Carley, Kenneth
Minnesota in the Civil War. Minneapolis: Ross and Haines, 1961
168 pp., illus

The book consists of a series of individual substantive essays which depict the role of the state in the war.

References: CWB II, 144.

13
Carter, Robert G.
Four Brothers in Blue. Washington: Gibson Brothers Press, 1913
xiii, 509 pp., front. (ports.).

Perhaps the best of the personal reminiscences, this volume, comprising letters written from the field by four Massachusetts brothers who served in the Army of the Potomac, provides a vivid picture of the life of a Union soldier. There is an accompanying narrative by the author.

A new edition containing an informative introduction by Frank Vandiver and a much needed index was published by the University of Texas Press, Austin, in 1978

References: CWB I, 67.

14
Catton, Bruce
The Army of the Potomac (3 volumes). Garden City: Doubleday and Company, 1951-53
maps, index.

Composed of three titles: *Mr. Lincoln's Army, Glory Road* and *A Stillness at Appomattox,* Bruce Catton's story of the Army of the Potomac is superb. In Volume 1 "...Catton takes the reader right into the Army of the Potomac..." (*Book Review Digest,* 1951). Henry S. Commager wrote of the second volume; "This second installment of the saga of the Army of the Potomac is better than its predecessor, *Mr. Lincoln's Army,* and that is high praise." (*Book Review Digest,* 1952). The final volume is an excellent presentation of the Virginia campaigns of 1864-1865. It won a Pulitzer Prize.

Other significant titles by this eminent historian include *This Hallowed Ground: The Story of the Union side of the Civil War* (Garden City, 1956) and *The Centennial History of the Civil War* (3 volumes, Garden City, 1961-1965.)

References: CWB I, 25; BCWL, 11; UBS 1, 3 p. 306; *Hallowed Ground:* CWB II, 7; BCWL, 6; *Centennial:* CWB II, 7; BCWL, 6.

LIFE

OF

DAVID BELL BIRNEY,

MAJOR-GENERAL

UNITED STATES VOLUNTEERS.

———⟨◆⟩———

PHILADELPHIA:
KING & BAIRD, 607 SANSOM STREET.

———

NEW YORK:
SHELDON & CO., 400 BROADWAY
1867.

15

Chamberlain, Joshua L.

The Passing of the Armies. New York: G. P. Putnam's Sons, 1915

xxi, 392 pp., front. (port).

In reviewing the Morningside Press Reprint (Dayton: 1974) in the February, 1976 issue of *Civil War Times Illustrated,* Albert Castel stated: "Chamberlain had a most successful military career capped by his being chosen to command the Union troops who were present when the Army of Northern Virginia lay down their arms. His account of the final Virginia campaign is superb. He was as great a writer as he was a fighter. No author ever has better conveyed that strange mixture of glory and tragedy of meaning and mystery felt by the armies of North and South as they passed off the stage of history. One of the classics of Civil War literature." Chamberlain commanded the Twentieth Maine Infantry and later a brigade in the Fifth Corps.

References: CWB 1, 68.

16

Cheek, Philip and Mair Pointon

History of the Sauk County Rifleman: Company "A", Sixth Wisconsin Veteran Volunteer Infantry. Madison: Democrat Printing Company, 1909

220 pp., front. plates, ports.

James I. Robertson states in *Civil War Books:* "One of the best company histories in Civil War literature; often quoted and justifiably so." The Sixth Wisconsin was one of the regiments that comprised the Iron Brigade in the Army of the Potomac.

References: CWB I, 69.

17

Coddington, Edwin B.

The Gettysburg Campaign: A Study in Command. New York: Charles Scribner's Sons, 1968

xv, 866 pp., maps, illus., index.

This volume has become the standard reference source not only for the battle but for the entire campaign. Robert D. Hoffsommer in his review of the book in *Civil War Times Illustrated* (1968) said: "Here at last is a book that states unequivocally - and proves it with dispassionate analyses - that Gettysburg was won by Meade."

A complete discussion of the second day's action around Little Round Top can be found in Oliver W. Norton's *The Attack and Defense of Little Round Top Gettysburg, July 2, 1863* (New York, 1913). Another superb description of the battle, especially on the third day, is Frank A. Haskell's *The Battle of Gettysburg* (Madison, 1908).

Coddington's book has been reprinted by Morningside Press (Dayton, 1979).

References: Norton: CWB I, 39; Haskell: CWB I, 31; BCWL, 12.

18
Cole, Arthur C.
The Era of the Civil War 1848-1870. Springfield: Illinois Centennial Commission, 1919
499 pp., front., ports., maps, index.
Highly valued by students of the war, this book contains a wealth of information about Illinois during the war years and has an excellent bibliography.
References: CWB II, 146; BCWL, 14.

19
Colton, Ray C.
The Civil War in the Western Territories, Arizona, Colorado, New Mexico and Utah. Norman, University of Oklahoma Press, 1959
ix, 230 pp., illus., ports., maps, index.
A complete study of the war in the western territories in which the author makes good use of source material to explain in detail the ramifications of the Union victory over the Confederacy and how it was accomplished.
References: CWB I, 25.

20
Conyngham, David P.
Sherman's March Through the South. New York: Sheldon and Company, 1865
431 pp.
A primary source for any study of Sherman's Atlanta and Carolina campaigns. The author, a reporter for the New York *Herald*, was a penetrating and perceptive observer.
References: CWB I, 73.

21
Crane, Stephen
The Red Badge of Courage. New York: D. Appleton and Company, 1895
233 pp.
The only piece of fiction included in this bibliography, Crane's book vividly portrays the war from the perspective of the common soldier. A perennial favorite, it sold ten thousand copies a year for over forty years, and remains a popular classic.
Many editions of this book, too numerous to list, have been printed since 1895.

22
Cunningham, Edward
The Port Hudson Campaign, 1862-1863. Baton Rouge: Louisiana University Press, 1963
174 pp., illus., index.

This monograph, the result of prodigious research and careful documentation, is a thorough treatment of the Union operation against this Confederate stronghold.

References: CWB I, 26.

23
Dana, Charles A.
Recollections of the Civil War. New York: D. Appleton and Company, 1898
xiii, 296 pp., front. (port.), index.

Originally a newspaperman, Dana worked directly for Secretary of War Stanton as a field reporter. He was with Grant for a significant period and his poignant observations are compellingly interesting.

References: CWB I, 78; BCWL, 15; UBS 1, 1, p. 73.

24
Davis, Oliver Wilson
Life of David Bell Birney, Major-General United States Volunteers. Philadelphia: King and Baird, 1867
xii, 418 pp., front. (port.), index.

Birney served with the Army of the Potomac from the Peninsular campaign until the siege of Petersburg. He rose in rank from lieutenant colonel to major general and was commanding the Tenth Corps when he died of malaria. His ably written biography is a basic source for any study of the Army of the Potomac.

References: CWB I, 79.

25
Dawes, Rufus R.
Service with the Sixth Wisconsin Volunteers. Marietta: E. R. Alderman and Sons, 1890
v, 330 pp., front., illus., port., index.

A standard source for the Iron Brigade. "Dawes' keen observations of the personal and intimate aspects of the Civil War and his extraordinary talent for writing in a fresh and vivid style make this one of the best of the regimental histories or personal memoirs ever written." *(Civil War History,* December, 1962).

A new edition, skillfully edited by Alan T. Nolan and containing an informative introduction and a critical bibliography, was published in 1962 (Madison: State Historical Society of Wisconsin for Wisconsin Civil War Centennial Commission).

References: CWB I, 79; BCWL, II.

26

Downey, Fairfax

Clash of Cavalry. New York: David McKay Company, 1959

xv, 238 pp., maps, illus., ports., index.

The definitive study of the Battle of Brandy Station, 9 June 1863. Civil War historians generally acknowledge that this largest cavalry engagement of the war demonstrated for the first time that Northern could defeat Southern cavalry, and gave the Union horsemen a confidence they never lost.

References: CWB I, 27.

27

Fleming, George Thornton, Editor

Life and Letters of General Alexander Hays. Pittsburgh: Privately Printed, 1919

viii, 708 (16) pp., front. (port.) plates, ports., index.

Another superb source book for information about the Army of the Potomac. Fleming skillfully edited the numerous letters of General Hays and supplemented them with notes obtained from data compiled by his son, Gilbert Adams Hays, to produce a valuable study.

References: CWB I, 89.

28

Ford, Worthington C., Editor

A Cycle of Adams Letters 1861-1865 (2 volumes). Boston: Houghton Mifflin Company, 1920

fronts., plates, ports., index.

Charles Francis Adams, U. S. Ambassador to the United Kingdom, was influential in policy discussion in the North as a result of his alarmist reports to Washington from London. Robert W. Johannsen comments in *Civil War Books:* "A valuable collection of the letters of C. F. Adams and his two sons, Charles Jr. and Henry; significant for their lucid comments of the economic, political and diplomatic developments of the war." In the same bibliography Norman Ferris said: "Selected wartime correspondence of the Adams family, stressing military intelligence but also revealing many facets of the American minister's diplomacy." The letters were masterfully edited by Ford.

A one volume edition was published by Kraus Reprint Company (New York: 1968).

References: CWB I, 253; CWB II, 56; BCWL, 14; UBS I, 1 p. 72.

29

Frassanito, William A.

Antietam: The Photographic Legacy of America's Bloodiest Day. New York: Charles Scribner's Sons, 1978

304 pp., maps, illus., index.

The author recreates the battle through original photographs. By documenting the photographer, date, and camera location for each view, Frassanito provides a definitive report on the Antietam photographs and highlights of Antietam's role as a landmark in the visual documentation of war, and provides the reader with a better understanding of the battle itself.

30
Frassanito, William A.
Gettysburg: A Journey in Time. New York: Charles Scribner's Sons, 1975
248 pp., maps, illus., index.

This volume makes history come vividly alive by its merging of text with the overwhelming reality of photographs. It is an absorbing and powerful volume and an example of analytical skill and meticulous historical research.

31
Freidel, Frank B., Editor
Union Pamphlets of the Civil War, 1861-1865 (2 volumes). Cambridge: Harvard University Press, 1967
index

These volumes offer superb examples of the verbal warfare that flourished behind Union lines during the Civil War. An introductory note by the author for each pamphlet plus an excellent essay on wartime propaganda and the various tract societies is also provided. E. B. Long said in his review (*The Journal of Southern History,* Volume 34, number 3, August 1968): "Now we have two quite massive 'source volumes' presenting in their entirety a carefully selected representative group of these tracts. The result is fortunate and a boon to Civil War scholarship. We expect these volumes will soon be cited in footnotes innumerable, enriching future Civil War history." Ludwell Johnson remarked in a review (*Virginia Magazine of History and Biography,* October, 1968): "It must be obvious that the present writer considers Professor Freidel's collection to be valuable and revealing."

32
Fuller, John F. C.
The Generalship of U. S. Grant. London: John Murray, 1929; First American edition: New York: Dodd, Mead, 1929
452 pp., index.

An imaginative and impressive analysis of Grant by a pre-eminent British military theorist and historian, this volume has been subjected to criticism specifically because of the author's inclination to rate Grant as the leading general of his age. Nevertheless, it is required reading for any study of Federal strategy, especially after Grant became Lieutenant General. Two companion volumes are the same author's *Grant and Lee: A Study in Personality and Generalship* (London: 1933; first American edition, Bloomington: 1957) and Carswell McClellan's *Grant Versus the Record* (Boston, 1887).

References: BCWL, 19; UBS 1, 2 p. 177; *Grant and Lee:* CWB II, 58; McClellan: CWB I, 36.

33
Gibbon, John
Personal Recollections of the Civil War. New York: G. P. Putnam's Sons, 1928
vii, 426 pp., maps, front. (port.).

The 1928 *Book Review Digest* contained the following quotations about Gibbon's work: "A volume of reminiscences which is one of the most readable and lifelike of any Civil War memoirs" and "a valuable addition to our knowledge of the Civil War." Gibbon was a superb artillery officer who, for a time, commanded the Iron Brigade. His memoirs are particularly revealing about Gettysburg.

The volume was reprinted by Morningside Press (Dayton, 1978).

References: CWB I, 93; BCWL, 16; UBS 1, 1 p. 73.

34
Gosnell, Allen H.
Guns on the Western Waters: The Story of the River Gunboats in the Civil War. Baton Rouge: Louisiana State University Press, 1949
xii, 273 pp., maps, illus., ports.

An authoritative and clear account of riverine operations during the war, this book presents an aspect of the Civil War which is more significant than generally recognized. Supplemental volumes include John D. Milligan's *Gunboats Down the Mississippi* (Annapolis: 1965) and Edwin C. Bearss's *Hardluck Ironclad: The Sinking and Salvage of the Cairo* (Baton Rouge: 1966, 1980).

References: CWB I, 224; BCWL, 13; UBS 1, 3 p. 306.

35
Grant, Ulysses S.
Personal Memoirs of U. S. Grant (2 volumes). New York: Charles L. Webster, 1885
maps, front. (ports.) plates, index.

Bruce Catton places Grant's memoirs on the top of his list of Civil War classics (*New York Times Book Review,* November 10, 1957). Ralph Newman states: "No Union list of personal narratives could possibly begin without the story of the victorious general. A truly remarkable work, not only in the military field, but as a work of literature, the book itself was the result of General Grant's last and greatest victory - his fight against death itself." See also Adam Badeau's *Military History of Ulysses S. Grant, 1861-1865* (New York: 1881), *Captain Sam Grant* by Lloyd Lewis (Boston: 1950), *Grant Moves South* and *Grant Takes Command* by Bruce Catton (Boston: 1960, 1968) as well as a recent publication, *Grant* by William S. McFeely (New York: 1981).

Another edition of Grant's *Memoirs* was published in 1895 (New York), and a one volume version proficiently edited with notes and introduction by E. B. Long (Cleveland: 1952).

References: CWB II, 59; BCWL, 16, UBS 1, 1 p. 72; Badeau: CWB I, 22; Lewis: CWB II, 72; BCWL, 19; UBS 1, 2 p. 177; Catton CWB II, 44; BCWL 19.

36

Gray, John C. and John C. Ropes

War Letters 1862-1865 of John Chipman Gray and John Codman Ropes. Boston: Houghton Mifflin Company, 1927

532 pp., ports (front.), index.

Both Bostonians, Gray was an officer while Ropes studied law during the war. One tells of active participation in the war while the other tells what he thinks of it. Their letters contain much that is instructive and valuable.

References: CWB I, 97.

37

Hammond, Bray

Sovereignty and an Empty Purse: Banks and Politics in the Civil War. Princeton: Princeton University Press, 1970

400 pp., index.

Describing in great detail the evolution of Northern financial policy, Hammond skillfully reveals the grave difficulties facing Lincoln and his Secretary of the Treasury, Salmon P. Chase, in raising funds, and shows that the Federal Government's ability to wage war depended heavily upon its financial base.

Other informative, amply researched volumes concerning Union finances during the Civil War include Sidney Ratner's *American Taxation, Its History as a Social Force in Democracy* (New York: 1942); *Money, Class and Party; An Economic Study of Civil War and Reconstruction* (Baltimore: 1959) by Robert Sharkey, and *A History of the Greenbacks, with Special Reference to the Economic Consequences of Thier Issue, 1862-1865* (Chicago: 1903) by Clair W. Mitchell.

References: Mitchell: CWB II, 132; Ratner: CWB II, 133; Sharkey: CWB II, 134.

38

Hammond, Harold E., Editor

Diary of a Union Lady 1861-1865. New York: Funk and Wagnalls Co., Inc., 1962

xlvii, 396 pp., index.

Allan Nevins remarks: "Mrs. Daly's diary, if read tolerantly and with a proper sense of humor, is endlessly entertaining" (from the Foreword). James I. Robertson in his review of the book in *Civil War History* (December, 1962) states "although heavily over-edited, a diary of outstanding quality—one no real student of the Civil War can henceforth overlook."

References: CWB II, 124.

BERDAN'S

United States Sharpshooters

IN THE

Army of the Potomac

1861-1865.

BY

CAPT. C. A. STEVENS,

(Historian.)

ILLUSTRATED.

Contentions fierce,
Ardent, and dire, spring from no petty cause.—SCOTT.

ST. PAUL, MINNESOTA.

1892.

39
Harrington, Fred Harvey
Fighting Politician: Major General N. P. Banks. Philadelphia:
University of Pennsylvania Press, 1948
xi, 301 pp., maps, port., index.

An authoritative life of a military amateur who achieved fame also as a fighting politician, this biography illustrates the role of the political general in the Civil War. J. G.
Randall commented: "*Fighting Politician* is the work of a keen student and a skillful
writer." *(Book Review Digest,* 1948).

A reprint edition was published by Greenwood Press (Westport, Connecticut) in 1970.

References: CWB II, 61; BCWL, 19; UBS 1, 2 p. 176.

40
Hayes, John D., Editor
Samuel Francis DuPont: A Selection from his Civil War Letters (3
volumes). Ithaca: New York, Cornell University Press, 1969
index

A model of professional editing by an American admiral, this work provides insight
into the character of one of the most influential officers in the Union navy as well as
valuable accounts of operations on the South Atlantic coast during the first two years
of the war. Eloquent and sophisticated, this member of the powerful DuPont family
reveals much in his correspondence about the important figures and issues of his day
and relations among members of the federal high command during the Civil War.

The only biography of Admiral DuPont is the somewhat outdated, but still useful,
Rear Admiral Samuel Francis DuPont by H. A. DuPont published by the National
Americana Society in 1926.

41
Hebert, Walter H.
Fighting Joe Hooker. Indianapolis: Bobbs-Merrill, 1944
368 pp., maps, front., illus., plates, ports., index.

The definitive study of the colorful Union general who commanded the Army of the
Potomac for six months including the Chancellorsville campaign, and who later
commanded two corps under Grant in the western theater. Hooker possessed a
divided personality that could inspire both devotion and hatred, and that could lead so
brilliantly and yet fail so ignominiously.

References: CWB II, 62; BCWL, 20; UBS 1, 2 p. 178.

42
Hesseltine, William B.
Lincoln and the War Governors. New York: Alfred A. Knopf, 1948
x, 405, xxii pp., index.

"An unsentimental survey of Lincoln's work in transforming inharmonious states into a solidified union," (Burton J. Hendricks, *Book Review Digest*, 1948). This volume contains analyses of various federal-state conflicts that enable the reader to appreciate Lincoln's shrewdness as a politician and wartime leader.

Reprinted in 1972 by Peter Smith (Gloucester, Massachusetts).

References: CWB II, 110; BCWL, 23.

43

Higginson, Thomas W.

Massachusetts in the Army and Navy During the War of 1861-1865 (2 volumes). Boston: Wright and Potter Printing Company, 1895-6

As William E. Parrish wrote in *Civil War Books,* this work is "The standard authority for Massachusetts' role in the war, at the front, and at home."

References: CWB II, 151.

44

Hinman, Wilbur F.

The Story of the Sherman Brigade. Alliance, Ohio: Published by author, 1897

xxxii, 33-1104 pp., illus., ports.

The Sherman brigade organized by John Sherman, later U. S. Senator and brother of General W. T. Sherman, was composed of the 64th and 65th Ohio Veteran Volunteer Infantry, the 6th battery of Ohio Veteran Volunteer Artillery and McLaughlin's Squadron, Ohio Veteran Volunteer Cavalry. The brigade saw action for four years in every major battle in the western theater. Hinman was lieutenant-colonel of the 65th Ohio Regiment. His exemplary story of the brigade is a basic source for the western theater of operations and contains many perceptive observations.

References: CWB I, 104.

45

Howard, Oliver O.

Autobiography of Oliver Otis Howard (2 volumes). New York: The Baker and Taylor Company, 1907

fronts., plates, ports., facsims., index

The reminiscences of one of the leading Union commanders who served in both the eastern and western theaters and later on the western frontier. Explaining how campaigns were fought and won or lost, Howard's recollection of detail was extremely accurate. These memoirs are an important source for any study of the Federal high command. An excellent supplemental volume is John A. Carpenter's *Sword and Olive Branch: Oliver Otis Howard* (Pittsburgh, 1964).

The autobiography was reprinted by Arno Press (New York) in 1973.

References: CWB I, 107; UBS 1, 1 p. 74; Carpenter: CWB II, 44.

46

Hyde, Thomas W.

Following the Greek Cross or Memoirs of the Sixth Army Corps.
Boston: Houghton Mifflin Company, 1894
xi 269 pp., front., plate, port.

A superior memoir by a Maine officer whose luminous remembrances provide an excellent description of army life in general and of the Sixth Corps in particular.

References: CWB I, 109; UBS 1, 3 p. 308.

47

Johnson, Ludwell H.

Red River Campaign: Politics and Cotton in the Civil War. Baltimore:
John Hopkins Press, 1958
317 pp., illus., index.

Based on extensive research, this book provides an interesting illustration of how military operations during the Civil War were often intimately interwoven with political, economic and ideological factors which frequently determined the time and place of a Union offensive. Johnson relates in vivid detail the various battles of the expedition.

References: CWB I, 33; BCWL, 12.

48

Jones, Edgar D.

Lincoln and the Preachers. New York: Harper and Row, 1948
xviii, 203 pp., ports.

John T. Hubbell in *Civil War Books* describes this volume as "a little known but revealing work on the varying relations between Lincoln and prominent Northern clergymen." Jones demonstrates that clergymen did not influence Lincoln any more than did lawyers, politicians, generals or diplomats. Lloyd Lewis remarked: "Lincoln's high morals and concepts of justice still appear to have come from his own conscience than from any person or group of persons" (*Book Review Digest,* 1948). A complementary volume is *From Flag to the Cross; or Scenes and Incidents of Christianity in the War* by Amos S. Billingsley (Philadelphia: 1872).

References: CWB II, 129; Billingsley: CWB II, 121.

49

Knox, Thomas W.

Camp-fire and Cotton-field: Southern Adventure in Time of War, Life with the Union Armies, and Residence on a Louisiana Plantation. New
York: Blelock and Company, 1865
524 pp., front., plates.

"A superb documentary on the Mississippi theater by a newspaper correspondent who seemed to stay 'in hot water' with most Federal commanders," commented James I.

Robertson in *Civil War Books*. Knox was employed by the New York *Herald*.
References: CWB I, 119.

50
Lamers, William M.
The Edge of Glory: A Biography of General William S. Rosecrans U.S.A. New York: Harcourt Brace and World, Inc., 1961
499 pp., illus., index.

A spirited and thorough attempt to correct the bad historical reputation of General Rosecrans. Fully documented and based largely on Rosecrans' personal papers, *The Edge of Glory* is the complete story of the much maligned general, and is important for the studies of the early fighting in western Virginia and the western theater, and for the relationship between politics and the military in the Federal high command.

References: CWB II, 70; BCWL, 21.

51
Leech, Margaret
Reveille in Washington 1860-1865. New York: Harper and Brothers, 1941
x, 483 pp., illus., (maps, facsim.) plates, index.

This Pulitzer Prize winner is the definitive story of life in the Federal capital during the Civil War, drawn mainly from contemporary accounts. A supplemental book is *The Symbol and the Sword; Washington D. C. 1860-1865* published by the Civil War Centennial Commission-District of Columbia (Washington: 1962).

References: CWB II, 154; BCWL, 23; UBS 1, 3 p. 306; *Symbol:* CWB II, 148.

52
Lewis, Loyd
Sherman: Fighting Prophet. New York: Harcourt Brace and Company, 1932
xii, 690 pp., front., illus. (maps, facsim.) plates, port., index.

The best biography of one of the most important Union figures. Carl Sandburg said of Lewis' effort "He had kinship with the Sherman spirit and wrote one of the supreme American biographies." Bruce Catton remarked that "Lloyd Lewis conveyed a warmth and immediacy which lifted *Sherman: Fighting Prophet* to a level which few twentieth century Northern accounts had attained" (*Book Review Digest*, 1932).

References: CWB II, 72; BCWL, 21; UBS, 1, 2 p. 179.

53
Logan, Mary S.
Reminiscences of a Soldier's Wife: An Autobiography, by Mrs. John A. Logan. New York: Charles Scribner's Sons, 1913
xvi, 470 pp., front., plates, ports., facsims.

One of the better accounts by a Northern woman. The wife of the Illinois general wrote her reminiscences with the familiar vividness of one who was a part rather than a spectator of events upon the stage of history. Included are lively and accurate sketches of famous figures that she knew intimately.

References: CWB II, 130; UBS 1, 3 p. 306.

54
Lonn, Ella
Foreigners in the Union Army and Navy. Baton Rouge: Louisiana State University Press, 1952
viii, 725 pp., port., index.

Immigrants accounted for approximately twenty percent of enlistments in the Union army. Professor Lonn has done an excellent job in completing this prodigious and definitive work.

The book was reprinted in 1969 by Greenwood Press (Westport, Connecticut).

References: CWB I, 10; UBS 1, 3 p. 306.

55
Lowenfels, Walter with the assistance of Nan Braymen
Walt Whitman's Civil War: Compiled and Edited from Published and Unpublished Sources. New York: Alfred A. Knopf, 1960
xvi, 333 pp., illus., index of poems.

"This anthology contains essays, excerpts from letters and forty-seven of Whitman's poems. With exceptional skill the editor has woven articulate prose and beautiful verses together into a literary drama that ranks with *John Brown's Body.* Whitman had the genius for kindling the spirit and emotions with his writing. His humane work in the Civil War is generally overlooked but was very significant" (*Civil War History,* September, 1961). David Donald said: "A realistic, personal and deeply touching account of the war as Whitman saw it" (*Book Review Digest,* 1961). Another volume which contains penetrating commentaries on humane work in the North is *Letters of a Family During the War for the Union* (2 volumes) compiled by Georgeanna Muirson (Woolsey) Bacon, (New Haven, 1899).

References: CWB I, 177; Bacon: CWB II, 120.

56
McClellan, George B.
McClellan's Own Story. New York: Charles L. Webster, 1887
xiv, 677 pp., illus., plates, maps, facsim., front. (port.), index.

This controversial Union general's memoirs are really an explanation of his wartime activities and decisions. McClellan's administrative and organizational skills are often overshadowed by his alleged shortcomings in the field and his involvement in party politics. It is seldom remembered that Grant used the weapon that McClellan forged to defeat Lee and win the war. Supplemental volumes include *George B. McClellan,*

The Man Who Saved the Union by H. J. Eckenrode and B. Conrad (Chapel Hill: 1941) and Peter S. Michie's *General McClellan* (New York: 1901).

References: CWB I, 124; CWB II, 73; BCWL, 17; UBS 1, 1 p. 74; Eckenrode: CWB II 54; UBS 1, 2 p. 78; Michie: CWB II, 76.

57

McClure, Alexander K.

Abraham Lincoln and Men of War Times. Philadelphia: The Times Publishing Company, 1892

462 pp., front. illus., plates, ports., facsims., index.

Paul M. Angle said that this volume is basic to understanding Lincoln and his age and that it is an uncommonly instructive book. He included it in his *A Shelf of Lincoln Books* (New Brunswick: 1946). McClure's reflections are reliable and offer an invaluable view of Lincoln's relations with key members of his administration. Other worthwhile volumes which discuss these relationships and their relevance include: *Inside Lincoln's Cabinet: The Civil War Diaries of Salmon P. Chase* edited by David Donald (New York: 1954) and *The Diary of Edward Bates, 1859-1866* edited by Howard K. Beale (Washington: 1933).

Lincoln and Men of War Times was edited by J. Stuart Torrey and reprinted in 1962 (Philadelphia: Rolley and Reynolds).

References: CWB II, 74; UBS 1, 1 p. 74; Donald: CWB II, 45; BCWL, 15; UBS 1, 1 p. 73; Beale: CWB II, 38; UBS 1, 1 p. 73.

58

May, George S., Editor

Michigan Civil War History: an Annotated Bibliography. Detroit: Wayne State University Press, 1961

xii, 128 pp.

A basic source for any study of Michigan's role in the war.

References: CWB II, 156.

59

Meade, George

The Life and Letters of George Gordon Meade (2 volumes). New York: Charles Scribner's Sons, 1913

fronts. (v. 1, port.), maps, index.

Meade, the hero of Gettysburg, was almost completely forgotten during the last year of the war because Grant made his headquarters with the Army of the Potomac of which Meade was the commander. A basic source for the Army of the Potomac, the general's letters reveal an eccentric, yet appealing, personality with a remarkably perceptive mind. They also contain penetrating evaluations of his military colleagues and of national political life. A good supplemental biography is Freeman Cleaves' *Meade of Gettysburg* (Norman: 1960).

References: CWB I, 129; BCWL, 21; UBS 1, 2 p. 178; Cleaves: CWB II, 46; BCWL 21.

HISTORY

OF THE

SAUK COUNTY RIFLEMEN

KNOWN AS

Company "A," Sixth Wisconsin Veteran
Volunteer Infantry

1861-1865

WRITTEN AND COMPILED
BY

PHILIP CHEEK
MAIR POINTON

1909

60

Miers, Earl S.

Web of Victory: Grant at Vicksburg. New York: Alfred A. Knopf, 1955

xiv, 320, xii pp., illus., ports., maps, index.

A well-written narrative of what many people consider the most important campaign of the Civil War. The fall of Vicksburg not only resulted in a divided Confederacy but it also provided the Federal forces with a victorious commander-in-chief. A companion volume is the recently published *The Final Fortress: The Campaign for Vicksburg, 1862-1863* by Samuel Carter III (New York: 1980).

References: CWB I, 37; BCWL, 12; UBS 1, 3 p. 307.

61

Monaghan, Jay

Civil War on the Western Border 1854-1865. Boston: Little, Brown and Company, 1955

x, 454 pp., index.

One of the most important volumes for understanding the complex situation on the western border. Bruce Catton in a review for the New York Times (*Book Review Digest,* 1955) said: "This solid, extensively documented book is a fine corrective for the works of the sentimentalists."

References; CWB I, 38; BCWL, 12; UBS 1, 3 p. 307.

62

Muffley, Joseph W.

The Story of Our Regiment. A History of the 148th Pennsylvania Vols. Des Moines: Kenyon Printing and Mfg., 1904

1096 pp., front., plates, ports.

The author relied heavily on personal incidents and commentaries to produce a regimental history that is widely consulted and highly regarded. The regiment was in the Second Corps, Army of the Potomac. It certainly belongs in any list of the best Union unit histories.

References: CWB I, 134.

63

Naiswald, L. Van Loan

Grape and Canister: The Story of the Field Artillery of the Army of the Potomac 1861-1865. New York: Oxford University Press, 1960

xiv, 593 pp., illus., maps, index.

The standard source for the type and employment of field artillery in the eastern campaigns. Bruce Catton complimented the volume by saying: "It does for the Army of the Potomac what Jennings Wise did for the Army of Northern Virginia with his *Long Arm of Lee.*"

References: CWB I, 39; BCWL, 14.

64

Nevins, Allan

Ordeal of the Union (8 volumes). New York: Charles Scribner's Sons, 1947-1971

illus., ports., maps, index,

This massive work is the most comprehensive study of the political, economic and social growth of the Nation between 1847 and 1865. The volumes dealing with the war (V-VIII) are a masterpiece. Nevins exhibits an absolute command of sources and writes in a superb style with penetrating analyses and deep insight. Arthur Schlesinger, Jr. commented on the first two volumes: "...this study will immediately take its place as the standard history of the eighteen-fifties." (*Book Review Digest,* 1948). A review of Volumes III and IV in *The New York Times Book Review* called them: "...a majestic peak in the mountains of American history." Together the eight volumes are the one indispensable source for any evaluation of the Northern view of the war and its causes. A fine one volume supplement is *The Divided Union* by J. G. Randall and D. Donald (Boston: 1961).

References: CWB II, 23; BCWL, 7; UBS 1, 3 p. 307; Randall: CWB II, 26; BCWL, 7.

65

Nevins, Allan, Editor

A Diary of Battle; The Personal Journals of Colonel Charles S. Wainwright 1861-1865. New York: Harcourt, Brace and World, 1962

549 pp., illus., index.

Wainwright was chief of artillery of the First Corps and later of the Fifth Corps in the Army of the Potomac. The editor described this unique and dramatic journal as "the most comprehensive and historically useful field diary by a Civil War officer that I have ever seen."

References: CWB I, 173; BCWL, 18.

66

Nichols, Edward J.

Toward Gettysburg: A Biography of General John F. Reynolds. University Park: Pennsylvania State University Press, 1958

x, 276 pp., illus., ports., maps, index.

The complete documented study of this perhaps finest of the Union Corps commanders who met an untimely death at Gettysburg. It is alleged that Reynolds turned down the chance to become commander of the Army of the Potomac prior to the position being offered to and accepted by Meade.

References: CWB II, 79; BCWL, 21.

HISTORY

OF THE

FIRST MAINE CAVALRY

1861–1865.

BY

EDWARD P. TOBIE.

PUBLISHED BY THE FIRST MAINE CAVALRY ASSOCIATION.

BOSTON:
PRESS OF EMERY & HUGHES,
No. 146 OLIVER STREET.
1887.

67
Niven, John
Connecticut for the Union; The Role of the State in the Civil War. New Haven: Yale University Press, 1965
xxiii, 493 pp., illus., facsim., maps, ports., index.

Allan Nevins wrote: "This well-stored and many sided volume offers materials upon which writers will be glad to levy. It contains instruction for the social historian, the economic historian and the military expert. One of the fullest, best proportioned and most penetrating of all the state records of the war." (from the Foreword).

References: CWB II, 159.

68
Nolan, Alan T.
The Iron Brigade: A Military History. New York: Macmillan, 1961
412 pp., illus., index.

The definitive study of one of the most famous brigades in the Union army. The work was fully researched and is expertly written.

Reprinted by the State Historical Society of Wisconsin in 1976.

References: CWB I, 138; BCWL, 12.

69
Oberholtzer, Ellis P.
Jay Cooke, Financier of the Civil War (2 volumes). Philadelphia: G. W. Jacobs and Company, 1907
fronts., illus., plates, ports., map, facsims, index.

The author had access to the documents and letters preserved by Cooke during his life, and used them well in writing this biography of a man whose value to the Union has been long ignored. Although not entirely objective, this book has real merit.

The book was reprinted by Augustus M. Kelley (Clifton, N. J.) in 1969.

References: CWB II, 79.

70
Page, Charles A.
Letters of a War Correspondent. Boston: L. C. Page and Company, 1899
xii, 397 pp., front., port., maps.

The letters of the chief reporter for the New York *Tribune* have been skillfully edited by James R. Gilmore. Page's observations and accounts of the fighting in the eastern theater are straightforward, yet exhilarating. A good reflection of the spirit of the age.

References: CWB I, 141.

71
Pepper, George W.
Personal Recollections of Sherman's Campaigns in Georgia and the Carolinas. Zanesville: H. Dunne, 1866
522 pp.

James Robertson comments in *Civil War Books*: "The highly revealing and reliable recollections of a journalist who served simultaneously as an officer in the 80th Ohio and a newspaper field correspondent."

References: CWB I, 145; UBS 1, 1 p. 74.

72
Porter, David D.
Naval History of the Civil War. New York: Sherman Publishing Company, 1886
xvi, 843 pp., illus., port., maps.

A primary source for the Union Navy's role in the Mississippi Valley theater of war. A great "story teller" like other members of his family, Porter is seldom truthful but always entertaining. The book is a valuable character study of America's "second admiral." Supplemental volumes include Porter's *Incidents and Anecdotes of the Civil War* (New York: 1885) and Richard S. West Jr.'s *The Second Admiral; A Life of David Dixon Porter, 1813-1891* (New York: 1937).

References: CWB I, 231; BCWL, 13, *Incidents*: CWB I, 148, 231; UBS 1, 1 p. 74; West; CWB I, 238; UBS 1, 2 p. 178.

73
Porter, Horace
Campaigning with Grant. New York: Century Company, 1897
xviii, 546 pp., front., illus., plates, ports., maps, facsim., index.

Porter served as Grant's aide and thus was able to observe the general close up. His poignant commentaries and his unpretentious views offer an excellent picture of the Union commander.

The book, edited by Wayne Temple, was reprinted by Indiana University Press (Bloomington) in 1961.

References: CWB I, 148; BCWL 17; UBS 1, 1 p. 74.

74
Pullen, John J.
The Twentieth Maine: A Volunteer Regiment in the Civil War. Philadelphia: J. B. Lippincott Co., 1957
338 pp., illus., index.

Bruce Catton, writing on Civil War literary classics of the Civil War in *The New York Times Book Review* (November 10, 1957), included Pullen's book. Catton remarked that "one need not actually have fought in the Civil War, apparently, in order to understand what it meant to the people who were in the middle of it." The author made excellent use of diaries, letters and other sources in writing this model regimental history. It is the best unit history of the Civil War.

Reprinted by Morningside Press (Dayton) in 1980.

References: CWB I, 149.

75

Quarles, Benjamin

The Negro in the Civil War. Boston: Little, Brown Company, 1953
xvi, 379 pp., illus., index.

This book surveys the service of Negroes in the Civil War in the military and behind the lines. Bruce Catton wrote: "Their story is a tragic one, and Professor Quarles tells it very well." (*Book Review Digest*, 1953). Two complementary books of much value are James McPherson's *The Negro's Civil War; How American Negroes Felt and Acted During the War for the Union* (New York: 1965) and Quarles' *Lincoln and the Negro* (New York: 1962).

References: CWB I, 213; BCWL, 23; UBS 1, 3 p. 307; McPherson: CWB I, 212; Quarles: CWB I, 213; BCWL, 23.

76

Randall, James G.

Lincoln the President (4 volumes). New York: Dodd, Mead Company, 1945-1955
illus., ports., maps, facsims., index.

A superb work, fascinating to read. "Randall was the undisputed academic authority on Lincoln. He had a mastery of the vast sources, monographic, documentary and manuscript, that make up the raw materials of Lincoln research. The volumes reflect his ability to analyze, collate and interpret these sources," wrote T. H. Williams. (*Book Review Digest,* 1955).

References: CWB II, 84; BCWL, 20; UBS 1, 2 p. 178.

77

Randall, James G.

Constitutional Problems Under Lincoln. New York: Appleton and Company, 1926
xviii, 580 pp., illus. (map), index.

Rodney C. Loehr commented in *Civil War Books:* "Perhaps the most underrated volume on the Civil War; absolutely indispensable to any study of Northern wartime politics." It is a comprehensive study of the relation of constitutional theory to administrative practice between 1861 and 1865.

A revised edition was published by the University of Illinois Press in 1951.

References: CWB II, 112; UBS 1, 2 p. 175.

78
Reed, Rowena
Combined Operations in the Civil War. Annapolis: Naval Institute Press, 1978
xxiii, 468 pp., illus., maps, ports., index.

The only full study of amphibious operations in the Civil War. Reed's book is a significant contribution to Northern Civil War history; a well written, amply documented narrative, which analyzes Union attempts to utilize combined operations to achieve success. E. B. Long described it as "a Civil War volume that has long been needed...a major contribution to broadening the military history of the war." (*Civil War Times Illustrated,* October, 1978). In this revisionist work, Professor Reed's arguments are stimulating and thought provoking.

79
Reid, Whitelaw
Ohio in the War: Her Statesmen, Her Generals, and Soldiers (2 volumes). Cincinnati: Moore, Wilstach and Baldwin, 1868
front., plate, port., map.

Although over one hundred years old, Reid's effort is still the most complete and accurate source of information about Ohio during the war.

References: CWB II, 161.

80
Sandburg, Carl
Abraham Lincoln: The War Years (4 volumes). New York: Harcourt, Brace and World, Inc., 1939
fronts., illus., maps, plates, ports., facsims., index at end of Vol. 4.

Bruce Catton, in his review of Civil War literature (*New York Times Book Review,* November 10, 1957) refers to Sandburg's effort as a "magnificent prose poem on Lincoln." Lloyd Lewis stated: "There has probably never been such a summoning of witnesses before in American literature or law, no such marshalling of incident, such collecting of evidence as the author here produces...It is all here..." (*Book Review Digest,* 1939).

References: CWB II, 87, BCWL, 20; UBS 1, 2 p. 178.

81
Shannon, Fred A.
The Organization and Administration of the Union Army 1861-1865 (2 volumes). Cleveland: The Arthur H. Clark Company, 1928
fronts. (port., vol. 2) plates, index.

James I. Robertson, commenting on the death of the author, said that his "two volume work remains indispensable." (*Civil War History,* June, 1963). Shannon's effort is the standard work on its subject.

Reprinted in 1965 (Gloucester: Peter Smith).
References: CWB I, 14; BCWL, 12; UBS 1, 3 p. 307.

82
Sheridan, Philip H.
Memoirs of P. H. Sheridan (2 volumes). New York: Charles L. Webster, 1888
fronts., illus., ports., maps, facsims., index.

One of the most important Union memoirs by a man who began the war as an infantry commander and became the commander of Union cavalry. Sheridan is often ranked with Grant and Sherman as the foremost Union commanders.

Another two volume edition, including an account of Sheridan's life from 1871 to 1881, by Michael V. Sheridan was published in New York in 1902.

References: CWB II, 88; BCWL, 17; UBS 1, 1 p. 75.

83
Sherman, William T.
Memoirs of W. T. Sherman (2 volumes). New York: D. Appleton and Company, 1875
map, index.

One of the most ambitious and eloquent of the Union generals, Sherman reveals as much about his own personality as he does about the war. Bruce Catton stated in his review of Civil War literature (*New York Times Book Review,* November 10, 1957): "Sherman's memoirs is a book that will survive as long as anyone is interested in the tragic convulsion of the Eighteen Sixties." He considered the volume a classic Civil War document. A penetrating supplemental volume is B. H. Liddell Hart's *Sherman; Soldier, Realist, American* (New York: 1929).

A second edition was published by D. Appleton in 1886. Other editions were published by Charles L. Webster (New York: 1892) and by Indiana University Press (1 volume) with a foreword by B. H. Liddell Hart (Bloomington: 1957).

References: CWB II, 89; BCWL, 17; UBS 1, 1 p. 75; Hart: CWB II, 72; BCWL, 21; UBS 1, 2 p. 179.

84
Smith, Edward C.
The Borderland in the Civil War. New York: Macmillan Company, 1927
412 pp., illus. (maps), index.

This volume demonstrates the importance of the "borderland" during the war. Smith included in that area the southern half of Ohio, Indiana, and Illinois as well as western Virginia, Kentucky and Missouri. Through extensive research he shows the decisive influence exercised by this section, the conditions by which it was affected, Lincoln's understanding of the political situation, and his wisdom in dealing with it. Several

UNDER THE MALTESE CROSS

ANTIETAM
TO
APPOMATTOX
THE LOYAL UPRISING IN
WESTERN PENNSYLVANIA
1861—1865

HUMPHREYS

SYKES—AYRES

GRIFFIN

CAMPAIGNS 155TH PENNSYLVANIA
REGIMENT
NARRATED BY THE RANK AND FILE

PUBLISHED BY
THE 155TH REGIMENTAL ASSOCIATION
PITTSBURG, PA.
1910

notable works useful in this area of study are *A History of West Virginia* by Charles H. Ambler (New York: 1933), *Politics in Maryland During the Civil War* by Charles B. Clark (Chestertown: 1952), *The Civil War and Readjustment in Kentucky* by E. Merton Coulter (Chapel Hill: 1926), *Delaware During the Civil War, A Political History* by Harold B. Hancock (Wilmington: 1961) *Just South of Gettysburg: Carroll County Maryland in the Civil War* edited by Frederic S. Klein (Westminister: 1963) and *Turbulent Partnership: Missouri and the Union* by William E. Parrish (Columbia: 1963).

References: CWB II, 163; Ambler: CWB II, 141; Clark: CWB II, 145; Coulter: CWB II, 147; Hancock: CWB II, 150; Klein: CWB II, 153; Parrish: CWB II, 160.

85

Soldiers and Sailors Historical Society of Rhode Island
Personal Narratives of Events in the War of the Rebellion (Series I-VII). Providence: Historical Society of Rhode Island, 1905-1915

These volumes contain superb, poignant, first-hand accounts by Federal soldiers and sailors. "The finest collection of monographs and short personal sketches in the field of Civil War memoirs." James I. Robertson, *Civil War Books* (Baton Rouge: 1967).

References: CWB I, 151.

86

Sommers, Richard J.
Richmond Redeemed: The Siege at Petersburg. Garden City: Doubleday and Company 1981
xxii, 670 pp., illus., maps, ports., index.

A well written narrative based on exhaustive research, this is a superb study of one segment of the siege of Petersburg when Grant had an opportunity to capture that city or Richmond in the fall of 1864. John Keegan of the Royal Military Academy in England described the book as "the most detailed study of a major military action ever written" (*Civil War Times Illustrated*, June, 1981).

87

Sparks, David S., Editor
Inside Lincoln's Army: The Diary of General Marsena Rudolph Patrick, Provost Marshal General, Army of the Potomac. New York: Thomas Yoseloff, 1964
536 pp., illus., ports., index.

An often overlooked primary source, Patrick's book contains keen perceptions recorded daily which offer an invaluable look at problems of discipline, morale, and military government during the Civil War.

References: CWB I, 142.

88

Sprague, Homer B.

History of the 13th Infantry Regiment of Connecticut Volunteers.
Hartford: Case, Lockwood and Company, 1867

viii, 362 pp., index.

This is one of the finest Federal unit histories. The Thirteenth Connecticut saw service
with the Nineteenth Army Corps in the Department of the Gulf and with the Army of
the Shenandoah later in the war.

References: CWB I, 162.

89

Starr, Stephen Z.

The Union Cavalry in the Civil War. Baton Rouge: Louisiana State
University Press, 1979

x, 509 pp., front., maps, illus., ports., index.

The first of a projected three volume work, this will be the definitive account of the
Federal cavalry in the war. Volume I is amply researched and fully documented and
reflects painstaking effort of the author to tell an accurate and complete story.

90

Steere, Edward

The Wilderness Campaign. Harrisburg: The Stackpole Company, 1960

522 pp., maps, index.

David Donald considered this book "a superb piece of technical military history
characterized by thoroughness, accuracy and insight." (*Book Review Digest,* 1961).
All of the action is presented with vigor and comprehensiveness. Steere did a fine job
with a difficult battle. A complementary work is Morris Schaff's *The Battle of the
Wilderness* (Boston: 1910).

References: CWB I, 44; Schaff: CWB I, 42; BCWL, 12.

91

Stevens, Charles A.

Berdan's U. S. Sharpshooters in the Army of the Potomac. St. Paul,
Minnesota: Privately Printed, 1892

xxiii, 555 pp., front., illus., plates, ports.

An absorbingly interesting account of one of the Northern army's elite units. A
journalist, Stevens gives an excellent narrative of events.

Reprinted in 1972 by Morningside Press.

References: CWB I, 162.

92

Stillwell, Leander

The Story of A Common Soldier of Army Life in the Civil War 1861-1865. Eric, Kansas: Press of the Erie Record, 1917

154 pp., front., ports.

Another overlooked important primary source. These recollections are comprehensive and they reveal the author's consistently perceptive powers of observation during his service in Company "D" Sixty-first Illinois infantry. James I. Robertson considered this volume "indispensable for any understanding of a Federal 'G. I.'."

A second edition was published by Franklin Hudson Publishing Company (Erie: 1920).

References: CWB I, 164.

93

Swanberg, W. A.

Sickles the Incredible. New York: Charles Scribner's Sons, 1956

xii, 433 pp., illus., ports., map, index.

Based on solid research and written with wit and gusto, this book is a fine biography of the complex and engimatic glory-seeking General Dan Sickles. David Donald comments that the "author has written a competent historical study based upon careful research. It is an entertaining addition to the shelf of Civil War biography" (*Book Review Digest,* 1956).

References: CWB II, 93; BCWL, 21.

94

Thomas, Benjamin P. and Harold M. Hyman

Stanton; The Life and Times of Lincoln's Secretary of War. New York: A. Knopf, 1962

xvii, 642 xii pp., illus., ports., facsim., index.

Although this project was originally started by the late Benjamin Thomas, who had done much research and organization, the completed biography is largely the work of Harold Hyman. The result is an exceptionally fine portrayal by two distinguished historians of one of the key figures in the Lincoln administration. It is also a fresh appraisal of Stanton's career that is scholarly in execution and exhaustive in detail.

References: CWB II, 94; BCWL, 21.

95

Thornbrough, Emma Lou

Indiana in the Civil War Era, 1850-1880. Indianapolis: Indiana Historical Bureau, 1965

xii, 758 pp., illus., facsims., ports.

A multivolume set. "Volume III deals with the war and contains a wealth of information on politics and society inside the Hoosier state," remarks William E. Parrish in *Civil War Books*.

References: CWB II, 164.

96
Tilley, Nannie E., Editor
Federals on the Frontier: The Diary of Benjamin F. McIntyre, 1862-1864. Austin: University of Texas Press, 1963
429 pp., illus, index.

McIntyre, who served in the Nineteenth Iowa Infantry in the Trans-Mississippi theater, was first a "noncom" and later a commissioned officer. His recollections are a revealing description of the day-by-day activities of soldier life. Jay Monaghan said that the book is "unusually well-edited, the author is a careful scholar who has thoroughly mastered the primary sources." (*Civil War History,* December, 1963).

References: CWB I, 126.

97
Tobie, Edward P.
History of the First Maine Cavalry, 1861-1865. Boston: Privately Published, 1887
xix, 735 pp., front., plates, port.

This is another first-rate unit history. The regiment, which saw action in the eastern theater primarily with the Army of the Potomac, suffered the highest casualties of any cavalry regiment in the Union army.

References: CWB I, 169.

98
Trefousse, Hans L.
Ben Butler: The South Called Him BEAST. New York: Twayne Publishers, 1957
365 pp., illus., index.

This volume is the best study of the most important of the Federal political generals. Bell I. Wiley in a review in *The New York Times* (*Book Review Digest,* 1957) summed up Trefousse's excellent objective effort as follows: "The author represents the stormy leader of Massachusetts as a brilliant lawyer, a smart politician and an able administrator. He adjudges him a patriotic, and in some respects effective supporter of the Union cause. He admits that Butler was opinionated, opportunistic, quarrelsome, cynical, and at times, extremely high-handed." Other good books on Butler are the *Autobiography and Personal Reminiscences of Major-General Benj. F. Butler; Butler's Book* by Benjamin F. Butler (Boston: 1892), Robert S. Holzman's *Stormy Ben Butler* (New York: 1954), and Richard S. West, Jr.'s *Lincoln's Scapegoat General: A Life of Benjamin F. Butler* (New York: 1965).

The Life of Billy Yank

The Common Soldier of the Union

BY

BELL IRVIN WILEY

THE BOBBS-MERRILL COMPANY

PUBLISHERS

INDIANAPOLIS   NEW YORK

References: CWB II, 95; Autobiography: CWB II, 43; BCWL, 15; UBS I, 1 p. 73; Holzman: CWB II, 65; BCWL, 21; UBS 1, 2 p. 177; West: CWB II, 100.

99

Tucker, Glenn

Chickamauga: Bloody Battle in the West. Indianapolis: Bobbs-Merrill, 1961

448 pp., illus., index.

Although Tucker did not write only about Union aspects of this battle, his effort is the best available. In a review in *Civil War History* (September: 1961), the author is complimented for telling the complete story in a skillful manner, and for portraying generals as well as lower ranks. Thomas' actions are especially well described, as is Rosecrans' reaction to the Confederate breakthrough.

A new edition has been published by Morningside Press (Dayton: 1972).

References: CWB I, 46.

100

Tucker, Glenn

Hancock the Superb. Indianapolis: Bobbs-Merrill, 1960

368 pp., illus., index.

R. N. Current said of this volume: "Tucker writes military biography as it should be written. He never loses his man - or his reader - in the details of campaigns and battles that have been often retold. Instead, he quickly makes the setting clear, then concentrates on Hancock's role. His prose is vivid, economical, and infused with scholarly and good sense." (*Book Review Digest:* 1961).

Reprinted by Morningside Press (Dayton: 1980).

References: CWB II, 95; BCWL, 20.

101

U. S. Navy Department

Civil War Naval Chronology, 1861-1865. Washington, D. C.: Naval History Division, 1971

1004 pp., illus., maps, ports., indexes.

An indispensable source of information about Civil War navies and naval operations, especially from the Union side, this huge volume contains not only day-by-day descriptions of events supported by excerpts from documents, memoirs and official reports, but hundreds of illustrations, maps, and plans. Also included are an informative introductory essay by two recent American admirals, lists of Civil War ships, and even a seventy page sheet music section of naval songs. In short, this book has everything for the sea-minded Civil War scholar or enthusiast.

References: CWB I, 236.

102

Van Deusen, Glyndon G.

William Henry Seward. New York: Oxford University Press, 1967

xi, 666 pp., illus., port., index.

Robert W. Johannsen wrote in *Civil War Books:* "By almost every standard [this is] the best biography of Lincoln's secretary of state; the product of exhaustive research." A supplemental volume is Frederic Bancroft's *The Life of William H. Seward* (New York: 1900).

References: CWB II, 97: Bancroft: CWB II, 38.

103

Van Horne, Thomas B.

The Life of General George H. Thomas. New York: Charles Scribner's Sons, 1882

x, 502 pp., front. (port.), maps, index.

In an unpretentious account of Thomas' role in the war, Van Horne convincingly argued that the General did not receive credit for his efforts and notable successes during the conflict. This biography is thoroughly researched and documented. Two later efforts are *Thomas: Rock of Chickamauga* by Richard O'Conner (New York: 1948) and *Rock of Chickamauga: Life of General G. H. Thomas* by Freeman Cleaves (Norman: 1948).

References: CWB II, 97; UBS 1, 2 p. 179; O'Conner: CWB II, 79; Cleaves: CWB II, 46; UBS 1, 2 p. 179.

104

Van Horne, Thomas B.

History of the Army of the Cumberland (3 volumes). Cincinnati: R. Clarke and Company, 1875

An exhaustive history of an often neglected major Federal army, the third volume is an atlas depicting the army's movements during its battles and campaigns.

References: CWB I, 47; BCWL, 12.

105

Warner, Ezra

Generals in Blue. Baton Rouge: Louisiana State University Press, 1972

xxiv, 680 pp., ports.

A basic research source for any study of Federal generals, Warner's compilation contains short but informative biographical sketches of each general supplemented by a photograph.

References: CWB II, 98.

106

Weber, Thomas

The Northern Railroads in the Civil War, 1861-1865. New York: King's Crown Press, 1952

318 pp., index.

There are several equally excellent books that demonstrate the significant contribution of the Northern rail network to the defeat of the Confederacy. Weber's book provides an excellent overview but not at the expense of necessary detail. Supplemental volumes include *Reminiscences of General Herman Haupt* (Milwaukee: 1901) by Herman Haupt, *Reports of Bvt. Brig. Gen. D. C. McCallum, Director and General Manager of the Military Railroads of the United States and (of James B. Fry) the Provost Marshall General* (2 volumes, Washington, 1866) by D. C. McCallum, Festus P. Summers' *The Baltimore and Ohio in the Civil War* (New York: 1939) and George E. Turner's *Victory Rode the Rails: The Strategic Place of Railroads in the Civil War* (Indianapolis: 1953).

References: CWB I, 19; Haupt: CWB I, 101; UBS 1, 1 p. 73; McCallum: CWB II, 137; Summers: CWB I, 15; Turner: CWB I, 15; UBS 1, 3 p. 307.

107

Weigley, Russell F.

Quartermaster General of the Union Army: A Biography of M. C. Meigs. New York: Columbia University Press, 1959

396 pp., illus., index.

A first-rate biography of one of the unsung Union figures. As Quartermaster General, Montgomery C. Meigs played a vital role in the Northern triumph. Weigley has produced a full study of the man responsible for feeding and transporting the Union armies. Earl S. Miers said "Weigley...writes with academic thoroughness" (*Book Review Digest,* 1960).

References: CWB II, 99; BCWL, 21.

108

Welles, Gideon

Diary of Gideon Welles (3 volumes). Boston: Houghton Mifflin, 1911 ports, index.

Welles' diary includes his years as Secretary of the Navy under Presidents Lincoln and Johnson. It contains a wealth of information on cabinet activities in general as well as naval affairs in particular. It is a necessary primary source for any study of the war in spite of the fact that Welles was opinionated and chronically critical of peers. Because of his sharp criticisms and caustic comments Welles decided to modify his diary prior to publication. Thus, the first edition is not the more reliable. The edition published by W. W. Norton and Company (3 volumes, New York: 1960) and edited by Howard K. Beale is better. A supplementary work is Richard S. West, Jr.'s biography *Gideon Welles: Lincoln's Navy Department* (Indianapolis: 1943).

References: CWB II, 99; BCWL, 18; UBS 1, 1 p. 75; West: CWB II, 99.

109
Whan, Vorin E.
Fiasco at Fredericksburg. Penn State: Penn State University Press, 1961
159 pp., illus.

In this incisive, scholarly study of the Union disaster at Fredericksburg, the author concentrates on the high command and analyzes the causes of the failure, rather than discussing the suffering of the soldiers in great detail.

References: CWB I, 48.

110
Whitman, Walt
Memoranda During the War. Camden: Privately Published, 1875-1876
68 pp., front. (ports.).

James I. Robertson commented in *Civil War Books:* "One of the most penetrating pictures of life and suffering in army hospitals; the famous Whitman wrote with powerful aplomb."

A reprinted volume edited by Roy P. Basler was published by Indiana University Press (Bloomington: 1962).

References: CWB I, 176.

111
Williams, T. Harry
Hayes of the Twenty-third; The Civil War Volunteer Officer. New York: Alfred A. Knopf, 1965
xii, 324, vi pp., illus., maps, ports., index.

The author produced a solid in-depth analysis of the volunteer officer and his regiment. Rutherford B. Hayes led the Twenty-third Ohio Volunteers and his experiences are a microcosm of a thousand other volunteer officers. Warren W. Hassler comments: "The subject emerges in sharp focus...the breadth and depth of the research, the dynamic mode of presentation, and the incisive evaluations make this book a genuine contribution to the study of American military history" (*Book Review Digest,* 1965).

References: CWB I, 179.

112
Williams, T. Harry
Lincoln and His Generals. New York: Alfred A. Knopf, 1952
viii, 363, iv pp., ports., map, index.

This is an important study by a leading historian. Allan Nevins called it "an able and fascinating book...although it presents the thesis of Lincoln's superior strategic grasp, it is not an argumentative volume. Rather it is a full-bodied and swift-paced narrative...the reader will gain a clear and shrewd overall comprehension of the Northern effort" (*Book Review Digest,* 1952). Robert S. Henry commented: "An admirably planned and executed work" (*ibid*).

References: CWB II, 33; BCWL, 12; UBS 1, 3 p. 308.

113
Williams, Kenneth P.
Lincoln Finds a General (5 volumes). New York: Macmillan Company, 1949-1959
ports., maps, index.

The irony of this hugely successful and prodigious undertaking is that the author could not take us to March of 1864 when Grant was promoted to commander-in-chief; death intervened before the final chapters were written. However, E. B. Long commented: "Williams has produced a comprehensive series for any true student of military history. His meticulous care for the facts, his trenchant and forthright mode of expression, his devotion to the best traditions of scholarly historical writing has made a solid and lasting contribution to Civil War literature" (*Book Review Digest,* 1960).

References: CWB I, 48; BCWL, 12; UBS 1, 3, p. 308.

114
Wiley, Bell I.
The Life of Billy Yank. Indianapolis: Bobbs-Merrill, 1952
454 pp., illus., ports., index.

Everything conceivable has been included in this encyclopedia of the Union soldier. The author drew extensively on primary sources, many of them unpublished. David Donald wrote: *"The Life of Billy Yank* is from every point of view an impressive achievement - a book of distinguished literary quality based on elaborate and careful research" (*Book Review Digest,* 1952).

The book was reprinted in limited edition by Louisiana State University Press (Baton Rouge: 1978).

References: CWB I, 178; BCWL, 23; UBS 1, 3 p. 308.

Part II

Regimental Histories

CONNECTICUT

115
Beecher, Herbert W.
History of the First Light Battery Connecticut Volunteers, 1861-1865
2 volumes
New York: A. T. De LaMare Printing and Publishing Co., 1901

Department of the South
Department of Virginia

ILLINOIS

116
Ambrose, D. Leib
History of the Seventh Regiment Illinois Volunteer Infantry
Springfield: Illinois Journal Co., 1868, 391 pp.

Army of the Tennessee

117
Fleharty, S. F.
Our Regiment: A History of the 102nd Illinois Infantry Volunteers
Chicago: Brewster and Hanscom, 1865, 192 pp.

Army of the Ohio
Army of the Cumberland

118
Howard, Richard L.
History of the 124th Regiment Illinois Infantry Volunteers...1862-1865
Springfield: H. W. Rokker, 1880, 519 pp.

Army of the Tennessee
Department of the Gulf

THE NAVAL HISTORY

OF THE

CIVIL WAR

BY

ADMIRAL DAVID D. PORTER, U. S. NAVY

ILLUSTRATED FROM ORIGINAL SKETCHES MADE BY REAR-ADMIRAL WALKE AND OTHERS

NEW YORK
THE SHERMAN PUBLISHING COMPANY
1886

119
Hubert, Charles F.
*History of the Fiftieth Regiment,
Illinois Volunteer Infantry in the War
for the Union*
Kansas City: Western Veteran Publishing
Co., 1894, 630 pp.

Army of the Tennessee

120
Kinnear, John R.
*History of the Eighty-sixth Regiment,
Illinois Volunteer Infantry*
Chicago: Tribune Company Book and Job
Printing Office, 1866, 148 pp.

Army of the Ohio
Army of the Cumberland

121
Regimental Committee
Ninety-second Illinois Volunteers
Freeport: Journal Steam Publishing House
and Book Bindery, 1875, 390 pp.

Army of Kentucky
Army of the Cumberland
Military Division Missis-
sippi

122
Sanford, Washington L.
*History of Fourteenth Illinois
Cavalry*
Chicago: R. R. Donnelly and Sons Co., 1898,
349 pp.

Department of the Ohio
Army of the Ohio

INDIANA

123
Brown, Edmund R.
*The Twenty-seventh Indiana Volun-
teer Infantry in the War of the Rebellion, 1861-1865*
Monticello: Privately Published, 1899,
640 pp.

Army of the Potomac
Army of Virginia
Army of the Cumberland

124
Floyd, David B.
History of the Seventy-fifth Regiment
of Indiana Infantry Volunteers, 1862-
1865
Philadelphia: Lutheran Publication Society,
1893, 457 pp.

Army of the Ohio
Army of the Cumberland

125
Smith, John T.
A History of the Thirty-First Regi-
ment of Indiana Volunteer Infantry
in the War of the Rebellion
Cincinnati: Western Methodist Book Con-
cern, 1900, 226 pp.

Army of the Ohio
Army of the Tennessee
Army of the Cumberland

126
Rowell, John W.
Yankee Artillerymen: Through the
Civil War with Eli Lilly's Indiana Bat-
tery
Knoxville: University of Tennessee Press,
1975, 320 pp., index

Army of the Ohio
Army of the Cumberland
Military Division Missis-
sippi

IOWA

127
Jones, Samuel C.
Reminiscences of the Twenty-second
Iowa Volunteer Infantry.
Iowa City: E. Hitchcock, 1907, 166 pp.

Department of Missouri
Department of Tennessee
Department of the Gulf
Army of the Shenandoah

128
Scott, William F.
The Story of a Cavalry Regiment: The
Career of the Fourth Iowa Veteran

Army of Southwest
   Missouri
Army of the Tennessee
Military Division Missis-
   sippi

FOUR BROTHERS IN BLUE

OR

Sunshine and Shadows of the War of the Rebellion

A STORY OF THE GREAT CIVIL WAR
FROM BULL RUN TO APPOMATTOX

BY

CAPTAIN ROBERT GOLDTHWAITE CARTER
U. S. Army, Retired

Formerly Private Company H, Twenty-second Massachusetts Volunteer Infantry (Henry Wilson Regiment); First Lieutenant, Fourth United States Cavalry; Brevet First Lieutenant and Captain, U. S. Army; a graduate of the United States Military Academy, Class of 1870; Awarded the Congressional Medal of Honor for "Most Distinguished Gallantry in Action with Indians," and two brevets, one for "Specially Gallant Conduct" in action with Indians and the "Grateful Thanks of the State of Texas, through its Legislature in Joint Assembly, for Prompt Action and Gallant Conduct, etc."

Captain Carter is a Companion of the Military Order of the Loyal Legion of the United States; A Companion of the Military Order of the Medal of Honor of the United States, Medal of Honor Legion; A Member of the Medal of Honor and Army and Navy Clubs of Washington, D. C., and United Service Club of New York. Corresponding Member of the Maine Historical Society and author of many monographs and short stories on Military Subjects in various papers and magazines, as well as Historical and Genealogical notes gathered from many sources.

WASHINGTON
PRESS OF GIBSON BROS., INC.
1913

State	Army and/or Department Served In

Volunteers
New York: G. P. Putnam's Sons, 1893, 602 pp., index

129
Smith, Henry I.
History of the Seventh Iowa Veteran Volunteer Infantry during the Civil War
Mason City: Mills and Co., 1903, 313 pp.

Army of the Tennessee

130
Sperry, Andrew F.
History of the 33rd Iowa Infantry Volunteer Regiment
Des Moines: Mills and Co., 1866, 237 pp.

Department of the Tennessee
Army of Arkansas

KANSAS

131
Starr, Stephen Z.
Jennison's Jayhawkers (7th Kansas Volunteer Cavalry)
Baton Rouge: Louisiana State University Press, 1973, 405 pp., index

Department of Kansas
Army of the Tennessee

KENTUCKY

132
Tarrant, Eastham
The Wild Riders of the First Kentucky Cavalry
Louisville: Privately Published, 1894, 503 pp.
New Edition: Lexington: Henry Clay Press, 1969, 503 pp., index

Army of the Ohio

133
Wright, Thomas J.
History of the Eighth Regiment Kentucky Volunteer Infantry
St. Joseph, Missouri: St. Joseph Steam Printing Co., 1880, 286 pp.

Department of the Ohio
Army of the Ohio

MAINE

134
Bicknell, George W.
History of the Fifth Regiment Maine Volunteers; June 24, 1861-July 27, 1864
Portland: Hall L. Davis, 1871, 417 pp.

Army of the Potomac

135
Gould, John M.
History of the First-Tenth-Twenty-Ninth Maine Regiment
Portland: Stephen Berry, 1871, 709 pp.

Army of the Potomac
Army of Virginia
Army of the Cumberland
Army of the Shenandoah
Department of the Gulf

136
Regimental Committee
The Story of One Regiment: The Eleventh Maine Infantry Volunteers in the War of the Rebellion
New York: Press of J. J. Little and Co., 1896, 505 pp.

Army of the Potomac
Department of North
   Carolina
Department of the South
Army of the James

137
Smith, John D.
The History of the Nineteenth Regiment of Maine Volunteer Infantry 1862-1865
Minneapolis: Great Western Printing Co., 1909, 356 pp.

Army of the Potomac

THE CAMPAIGN

OF

CHANCELLORSVILLE

A STRATEGIC AND
TACTICAL STUDY

BY

JOHN BIGELOW, Jr.

MAJOR U. S. ARMY, RETIRED

AUTHOR OF "MARS-LA-TOUR AND GRAVELOTTE," "THE PRINCIPLES
OF STRATEGY," AND "REMINISCENCES OF THE
SANTIAGO CAMPAIGN "

WITH MAPS AND PLANS

NEW HAVEN: YALE UNIVERSITY PRESS
LONDON: HENRY FROWDE
OXFORD UNIVERSITY PRESS

MASSACHUSETTS

138
Bruce, George A.
The Twentieth Regiment of Massachusetts Volunteer Infantry
Boston: Houghton, Mifflin and Co., 1906, 519 pp.

Army of the Potomac

139
Cudworth, Warren H.
History of the First Regiment (Massachusetts Infantry)
Boston: Walker, Fuller and Co., 1866, 528 pp.

Army of the Potomac

140
Davis, Charles E.
Three Years in the Army: The Story of the Thirteenth Massachusetts Volunteers, July, 1861-August, 1864
Boston: Estes and Lauriat, 1894, 476 pp., index

Army of the Potomac
Army of Virginia

141
Derby, W. P.
Bearing Arms in the Twenty-Seventh Massachusetts Regiment Volunteer Infantry During the Civil War
Boston: Wright and Potter Printing Co., 1883, 607 pp., index

Department of North
Carolina
Army of the Potomac

142
Ewer, James K.
The Third Massachusetts Cavalry in the War for the Union
Maplewood: William G. J. Perry, 1903, 565 pp.

Army of the Gulf
Department of the Gulf
Army of the Shenandoah

143
Howe, Henry W.
Passages From the Life of Henry Warren Howe...A Condensed History of the Thirtieth Massachusetts Regiment
Lowell: Courier-citizen Co., 1899, 211 pp.

Department of the Gulf
Army of the Shenandoah

144
Johns, Henry T.
Life with the Forty-Ninth Massachusetts Volunteers
Pittsfield: C. A. Alvord Press, 1864, 391 pp.

Department of the Gulf

145
Lincoln, William S.
Life with the Thirty-Fourth Massachusetts Infantry in the War of the Rebellion
Worcestor: Noyes, Snow and Co., 1879, 477 pp.

Department of Washington
Department of West Virginia
Army of the James

146
Moors, John F.
History of the Fifty-second Regiment Massachusetts Volunteers
Boston: George H. Ellis Press, 1893, 268 pp.
Second Edition: Washington, D. C., 1890, 435 pp.

Department of the Gulf

147
Parker, John L.
Henry Wilson's Regiment, History of the Twenty-second Massachusetts Infantry, the Second Company Sharpshooters and the Third Light Battery

Army of the Potomac

THE STORY

OF THE

SHERMAN BRIGADE.

THE CAMP, THE MARCH, THE BIVOUAC, THE BATTLE;
AND HOW "THE BOYS" LIVED AND DIED
DURING FOUR YEARS OF ACTIVE
FIELD SERVICE.

Sixty-fourth Ohio Veteran Volunteer Infantry.
Sixty-fifth Ohio Veteran Volunteer Infantry.
Sixth Battery, Ohio Veteran Volunteer Artillery.
McLaughlin's Squadron, Ohio Veteran Volunteer Cavalry.

WITH 368 ILLUSTRATIONS.

No rumor of the foe's advance
  Now swells upon the wind;
No troubled thought at midnight haunts
  Of loved ones left behind.
No vision of the morrow's strife
  The soldier's dream alarms;
No braying horn or screaming fife
  At dawn shall call to arms.
          —*Theodore O'Hara.*

BY

WILBUR F. HINMAN,

Late Lieutenant-colonel, Sixty-fifth Ohio Regiment; Author of
"Corporal Si Klegg and His Pard," etc.

PUBLISHED BY THE AUTHOR.
1897.

Boston: Published by Regimental
Association, 1887, 591 pp.

148
Putnam, Samuel H.
The Story of Company "A" Twenty-fifth Regiment; Massachusetts Volunteers
Worcestor: Putnam Davis and Co., 1886
325 pp.

Department of North
Carolina

149
Regimental Committee
History of the Fifth Massachusetts Battery
Boston: Luther E. Cowles, 1902, 991 pp.,
index

Army of the Potomac

150
Regimental Committee
History of the Thirty-Fifth Regiment Massachusetts Volunteers
Boston: Mills, Knight and Co., 1884, 475 pp.

Army of the Potomac
Army of the Tennessee

151
Roe, Alfred S., and Charles Nutt
History of the First Regiment of Heavy Artillery Massachusetts Volunteers
Worcestor: Published by Regimental Association, 1917, 507 pp., index

Department of Washington
Army of the Potomac

152
Roe, Alfred S.
*The Fifth Regiment Massachusetts
Volunteer Infantry*
Boston: Published by Fifth Regiment Veteran
Association, 1909, 535 pp., index

Army of Northeast Virginia
Department of North
   Carolina
Middle Department

153
Roe, Alfred S.
*The Tenth Regiment Massachusetts
Volunteer Infantry*
Springfield: Published by Tenth Regiment
Veteran Association, 1909, 535 pp., index

Army of the Potomac

154
Stevens, William B.
*History of the Fiftieth Regiment of
Infantry Massachusetts Volunteer
Militia in the Late War of the Rebel-
lion*
Boston: Griffith-Stillings Press, 1907, 399 pp.

Department of the Gulf

MICHIGAN

155
Curtis, Orson B.
*History of the Twenty-fourth Michi-
gan of the Iron Brigade*
Detroit: Winn and Hammond, 1891, 483 pp.

Army of the Potomac

156
Thatcher, Marshall P.
*A Hundred Battles in the West; Sec-
ond Michigan Cavalry*
Detroit: Published by author, 1884, 490 pp.

Army of Mississippi
Army of the Cumberland

NEW HAMPSHIRE

157
Buffum, Francis
A Memorial of the Great Rebellion, being a History of the Fourteenth Regiment New Hampshire Volunteers
Boston: Rand Avery and Company, 1882, 443 pp.

Military District of
  Washington
Department of the Gulf
Army of the Shenandoah

158
Cadwell, Charles K.
The Old Sixth Regiment, Its War Record 1861-5
New Haven: Tuttle, Morehouse and Taylor, 1875, 227 pp.

Department of North
  Carolina
Army of the Potomac
Army of the Tennessee

159
Child, William
A History of the Fifth Regiment New Hampshire Volunteers in the Civil War
Bristol: R. W. Musgrove, 1893, 564 pp.

Army of the Potomac

160
Haynes, Martin A.
History of the Second Regiment New Hampshire Volunteers
Manchester: Charles F. Livingston, 1865 232 pp.
Second Edition: Lakeport, 1896, 350 pp.

Army of the Potomac
Army of the James

161
Little, Henry F. W.
The Seventh Regiment New Hampshire Volunteers in the War of the

District of Florida
Department of the South
Army of the James

48

Rebellion

Concord: Published by Seventh New Hampshire Veteran Association, 1896, 700 pp.

162

Thompson, S. Millet

Thirteenth Regiment of New Hampshire Volunteer Infantry

Boston: Houghton, Mifflin and Co., 1888, 717 pp.

Army of the Potomac
Department of Virginia
Army of the James

NEW JERSEY

163

Baquet, Camille

History of the First Brigade, New Jersey Volunteers

Trenton: Published by the State of New Jersey, 1910, 515 pp.

Army of the Potomac
Army of the Shenandoah

164

Pyne, Henry R.

The History of the First New Jersey Cavalry

Trenton: J. A. Beecher, 1871, 350 pp.

New Edition: *Ride to War: History of the First New Jersey Cavalry* edited by Earl S. Miers

New Brunswick: Rutgers University Press, 1961, 340 pp.

Army of the Potomac
Army of Virginia

165

Terrell, John N.

Campaign of the Fourteenth Regiment New Jersey Volunteers

Middle Department
Army of the Potomac
Army of the Shenandoah

49

New Brunswick: Terhune & Van Anglen's
Press, 1866, 132 pp.

Another Edition: New Brunswick: Daily
Home News Press, 1884, 132 pp.

NEW YORK

166
Beach, William H.
*The First New York (Lincoln)
Cavalry*
New York: The Lincoln Cavalry Association,
1902, 579 pp.

Army of the Potomac
Middle Department
Army of West Virginia

167
Clark, James H.
*The Iron Hearted Regiment: 115th
Regiment New York Volunteers*
Albany: J. Munsell, 1865, 337 pp.

Department of the South
District of Florida
Army of the James
Department of North
      Carolina

168
Clark, Orton S.
*The One Hundred and Sixteenth
Regiment of New York State
Volunteers*
Buffalo: Printing House of Matthews and
Warren, 1868, 361 pp.

Department of the Gulf
Army of the Shenandoah

169
Collins, George K.
*Memoirs of the 149th Regiment New
York Volunteer Infantry*
Syracuse: Published by author, 1891, 426 pp.

Army of the Potomac
Army of the Cumberland

EDWIN B. CODDINGTON

THE GETTYSBURG CAMPAIGN

A Study in Command

CHARLES SCRIBNER'S SONS · NEW YORK

170
Davenport, Alfred
Camp and Field Life of the Fifth New York Volunteer Infantry
New York: Dick and Fitzgerald, 1879, 485 pp.

Army of the Potomac

171
Floyd, Fred C.
History of the 40th (Mozart) Regiment New York State Volunteers
Boston: F. H. Gilson Co., 1909, 468 pp.

Army of the Potomac

172
Hanaburgh, D. H.
History of the 128th Regiment, New York Volunteers
Pokeepsee: Enterprise Publishing Co., 1894, 280 pp., index

Department of the Gulf
Army of the Shenandoah

173
Jaques, John W.
Three Years' Campaign of the Ninth New York State Militia (83rd New York Infantry)
New York: Hilton and Co., 1865, 248 pp.

Department of North
  Carolina
Army of the Potomac
Department of Virginia

174
Morris, Gouverneur
The History of a Volunteer Regiment...the Sixth Regiment New York Volunteer Infantry...1861-1865
New York: Veteran Volunteer Publishing Co., 1891, 160 pp.

Department of the South
Department of the Gulf

175
Pellet, Elias P.
History of the 114th Regiment, New

Middle Department
Department of the Gulf
Army of the Shenandoah

State	Army and/or Department Served In

York State Volunteers
Norwich: Telegraph and Chronicle Power Press Print, 1866, 406 pp.

176
Roe, Alfred S.
The Ninth New York Heavy Artillery
Worcestor, Massachusetts: Published by the author, 1899, 615 pp.

Army of the Potomac
Department of Washington
Army of the Shenandoah

177
Stevenson, James H.
Boots and Saddles (First New York Cavalry)
Harrisburg: Patriot Publishing Co., 1879, 388 pp.

Army of the Potomac
Middle Department
Army of West Virginia

178
Todd, William
The Seventy-ninth Highlanders New York Volunteers
Albany: Press of Brandow, Barton and Co., 1886, 513 pp.

Army of the Potomac
Department of the South
Army of the Ohio
Army of the Tennessee

OHIO

179
Chamberlin, W. H.
History of the Eighty-first Regiment Ohio Infantry Volunteers, during the War of the Rebellion
Cincinnati: Gazette Steam Printing House, 1865, 198 pp.

Army of the Tennessee

180
Curry, William L.
Four Years in the Saddle. History of the First Ohio Volunteer Cavalry
Columbus: Champlin Printing Co., 1898, 470 pp.

Army of the Ohio
Army of the Cumberland
Military Division Mississippi

181
Hannaford, Ebenezer
The Story of a Regiment: A History of the Campaigns...of the Sixth Regiment Ohio Volunteer Infantry
Cincinnati: Published by the author, 1868, 639 pp.

Army of the Ohio
Army of the Cumberland

182
Hurst, Samuel H.
Journal History of the Seventy-Third Ohio Volunteer Infantry
Chillicothe: Privately Published, 1866, 639 pp.

Department of the
  Mountains
Army of Virginia
Army of the Potomac
Army of the Cumberland

183
Kepler, William
History of the Three Months' and Three Years' Service...of the Fourth Regiment Ohio Volunteer Infantry
Cleveland: Leader Printing Co., 1886, 287 pp.

Army of the Potomac
Department of the
  Rappahannock

184
Keyes, Charles M.
The Military History of the 123rd Regiment of Ohio Volunteer Infantry
Sandusky: Register Steam Press, 1874, 196 pp.

Middle Department
Department of West
  Virginia
Army of the James

CIVIL WAR NAVAL CHRONOLOGY

1861–1865

Compiled by

Naval History Division
Navy Department

Washington: 1971

185
McAdams, F. M.
*Everyday Soldier Life or A History of
the One Hundred and Thirteenth
Ohio Volunteer Infantry*
Columbus: Charles M. Cott and Co., 1884,
400 pp.

Army of the Cumberland
Army of Kentucky

186
Mason, F. H.
The Forty-second Ohio Infantry
Cleveland: Cobb, Andrews and Co., 1876,
306 pp.

Army of the Ohio
Army of the Tennessee
Department of the Gulf

PENNSYLVANIA

187
Bosbyshell, Oliver C.
*The 48th in the War: Campaigns of
the 48th Regiment Infantry Pennsylvania Veteran Volunteers*
Philadelphia: Avil Printing Co., 1895,
205 pp., index

Department of North
    Carolina
Army of the Potomac
Army of the Ohio

188
Chamberlin, Thomas
*History of the 150th Regiment Penn-
sylvania Volunteers*
Philadelphia: J. P. Lippincott Co., 1895,
277 pp.
Another Edition: Philadelphia, F. McManus,
Jr. & Co., 1905, 362 pp., index

Army of the Potomac

189
History of the One Hundred Forty-first Regiment, Pennsylvania Volunteers 1862-1865

Towanda: Published by author, 1885, 274 pp. index

Army of the Potomac

190
Davis, William W. H.
History of the 104th Pennsylvania Regiment from August 1861 to September 1864

Philadelphia: J. P. Rogers, 1866, 373 pp.

Army of the Potomac
Department of the South
Army of the Shenandoah

191
Dornblaser, T. F.
Sabre Strokes of the Pennsylvania Dragoons in the War of 1861-1865 (7th Pennsylvania Cavalry)

Philadelphia: Lutheran Publication Society, 1884, 273 pp.

Army of the Ohio
Army of the Cumberland
Military Division Mississippi

192
Glover, Edwin A.
Bucktailed Wildcats (150th Regiment Pennsylvania Volunteers)

New York: Thomas Yoseloff, 1960, 328 pp., index

Army of the Potomac

193
Hays, Gilbert A.
Under the Red Patch: Story of the Sixty-third Regiment Pennsylvania Volunteers

Pittsburgh: Published by 63rd Regimental Association, 1908, 479 pp.

Army of the Potomac

The
Twentieth
Maine

A VOLUNTEER REGIMENT
IN THE CIVIL WAR

BY

John J. Pullen

J. B. LIPPINCOTT COMPANY
PHILADELPHIA AND NEW YORK

194
Judson, Amos M.
History of the Eighty-third Regiment Pennsylvania Volunteers
Erie: B. F. H. Lynn, 1865, 159 pp.

Army of the Potomac

195
Mulholland, St. Clair A.
The Story of the 116th Regiment Pennsylvania Infantry
Philadelphia: F. McManus, Jr. and Co., 1899, 422 pp.
Another Edition: Philadelphia: F. McManus, Jr., 1903, 462 pp.

Army of the Potomac

196
Parker, Thomas H.
History of the 51st Regiment of P. V. and V. V. 1861-1865
Philadelphia: King and Baird, 1869, 712 pp.

Department of North
   Carolina
Army of the Potomac
Army of the Ohio

197
Regimental History Committee
History of the Third Pennsylvania Cavalry 1861-1865
Philadelphia: Philadelphia-Franklin Printing Co., 1905, 614 pp.

Army of the Potomac

198
Rowell, John W.
Yankee Cavalrymen-Through the Civil War with the Ninth Pennsylvania Cavalry
Knoxville: University of Tennessee Press, 1971, 280 pp., index

Army of the Ohio
Department of the
   Cumberland
Military Division Missis-
   sippi

199
Sprenger, George F.   Army of the Potomac
*Concise History of the Camp and
Field Life of the 122nd Regiment,
Pennsylvania Volunteers*
Lancaster: The New Era Steam Book Print,
1885, 380 pp.

200
Survivor's Association   Army of the Potomac
*History of the Corn Exchange Regi-
ment, 118th Pennsylvania Volunteers*
Philadelphia: J. L. Smith, 1888, 746 pp.

Another Edition: *Antietam to Appomattox
with the 118th Pennsylvania Volunteers Corn
Exchange Regiment*
Philadelphia: J. L. Smith, 1892, 746 pp.

Another Edition: *History of the 118th Pennsylvania Volunteers Corn Exchange Regiment.*
Philadelphia: J. L. Smith, 1905, 743 pp.

201
Under the Maltese Cross, Campaigns   Army of the Potomac
of the 155th Pennsylvania Volunteers
Narrated by the Rank & File
Pittsburgh: Published by the 155th Regi-
mental Association, 1910, 817 pp.

202
Vautier, John D.   Army of Virginia
History of the 88th Pennsylvania   Army of the Potomac
Regiment Volunteers
Philadelphia: J. P. Lippincott Co., 1894.
280 pp.

State	Army and/or Department Served In

203
Westbrook, Robert S.
History of the 49th Pennsylvania Volunteers
Altoona: Altoona Times Print, 1898, 279 pp.

Army of the Potomac
Army of the Shenandoah

204
Wilson, Suzanne C.
Column South with the 15th Pennsylvania Cavalry
Flagstaff, Arizona: J. F. Colton and Co., 1960, 414 pp., index

Army of the Potomac
Army of the Cumberland
Military Division Mississippi

RHODE ISLAND

205
Allen, George H.
Forty-Six Months with the Fourth Rhode Island Volunteers in the War of 1861-1865
Providence: J. A. and R. A. Reid, 1887, 389 pp.

Army of the Potomac
Department of North Carolina

206
Burlingame, John K.
History of the Fifth Regiment of Rhode Island Heavy Artillery During Three Years and a Half of Service in North Carolina
Providence: Snow and Farnham, 1892, 382 pp.

Department of North Carolina

207
Denison, Frederic
Sabres and Spurs: The First Regiment Rhode Island Cavalry in the Civil War

Army of the Potomac
Army of Virginia
Army of the Shenandoah

PERSONAL RECOLLECTIONS

OF

SHERMAN'S CAMPAIGNS.

IN

GEORGIA

AND THE

CAROLINAS.

BY CAPT. GEORGE W. PEPPER.

ZANESVILLE, OHIO:
PUBLISHED BY HUGH DUNNE,
NORTH FOURTH ST., ADJOINING COURT HOUSE,
1866.

Central Falls: Published by First Rhode Island Cavalry Veteran Association, 1876, 599 pp.

208
Denison, Frederic
Shot and Shell: The Third Rhode Island Heavy Artillery in the Rebellion
Providence: J. A. and R. A. Reid, 1879, 368 pp.

Department of the South
Department of North
    Carolina

209
Rhodes, John H.
The History of Battery B, First Regiment Rhode Island Light Artillery in the War to Preserve the Union
Providence: Snow and Farnham, 1894, 406 pp.

Army of the Potomac
Army of the Shenandoah
Department of North
    Carolina

TENNESSEE

210
Carter, W. R.
History of the First Regiment of Tennessee Volunteer Cavalry in the Great War of the Rebellion
Knoxville: Gaut-Ogden, 1902, 335 pp.

Army of the Cumberland
Military Division Mississippi

VERMONT

211
Benedict, George G.
Vermont in the Civil War: A History of the Part Taken by the Vermont Soldiers and Sailors in the War for the Union 1861-1865 (2 volumes)

Burlington: Free Press Association, 1886-
1888, index.

WISCONSIN

212
Bryant, Edwin E.   Army of the Potomac
History of the Third Regiment of Wis-   Army of Virginia
consin Veteran Volunteer Infantry   Army of the Cumberland
Madison: Published by Veteran Association
of Regiment, 1891, 445 pp.

FEDERAL TROOPS

213
Higginson, Thomas W.   Department of the South
Army Life in a Black Regiment (33rd
Infantry United States Colored
Troops)
Boston: Fields, Osgood and Company, 1870,
296 pp.
New Edition: Boston: Houghton, Mifflin and
Company, 1900, 413 pp.
Another Edition: East Lansing: Michigan
State University Press, 1960, 235 pp.

JAY COOKE

FINANCIER OF THE CIVIL WAR

by

ELLIS PAXSON OBERHOLTZER, Ph. D.,

AUTHOR OF "ROBERT MORRIS, PATRIOT AND FINANCIER," "ABRAHAM
LINCOLN," ETC.

VOLUME ONE

PHILADELPHIA

GEORGE W. JACOBS & CO.

PUBLISHERS

Part III

Participant Accounts

214
Agassiz, George R., Editor
*Meade's Headquarters 1863-1865;
Letters of Colonel Theodore Lyman
from the Wilderness to Appomattox*
Boston: Atlantic Monthly Press, 1922, 371
pp.

New Edition: Freeport, New York: Books for
Libraries, 1970, 371 pp.

Army of the Potomac

215
Angle, Paul M., Editor
*Three Years in the Army of the Cum-
berland; The Letters and Diary of
Major James A. Connolly* (123rd Il-
linois Infantry)
Bloomington: Indiana University Press, 1959,
399 pp.

Reprinted: New York: Kraus Reprint Co.,
1969, 399 pp.

Army of the Cumberland

216
Beatty, John
The Citizen Soldier (3rd Ohio Infan-
try)
Cincinnati: Wilstach, Baldwin Company,
1879, 401 pp.

New Edition: *Memoirs of a Volunteer, 1861-
1863*
edited by Harvey S. Ford
New York: W. W. Norton and Company,
Inc., 1946, 317 pp.

Army of the Ohio
Army of the Cumberland

217
Bellard, Alfred
Gone for a Soldier (5th New Jersey
Infantry)
Boston: Little Brown & Co., 1975, 298 pp.,
index

Army of the Potomac

218
Benedict, George G.
Army Life in Virginia. Letters from Twelfth Vermont Regiment and Personal Experiences of Volunteer Service in the War for the Union 1862-1863
Burlington: Free Press Association, 1895, 194 pp.

District of Washington
Army of the Potomac

219
Clark, J. S.
Life in the Middle West; Reminiscences of J. S. Clark (1st and 34th Iowa Infantry)
Chicago: The Advance Publishing Co., 1916, 226 pp.

Department of Tennessee
Army of the Tennessee
Department of the Gulf

220
Cronin, David E.
The Evolution of a Life, Described in the Memoirs of Major Seth Eyland (pseud.) (1st New York Mounted Rifles)
New York: S. W. Green's Son Co., 1884, 336 pp.

Department of Virginia and
North Carolina

221
Eby, Cecil D., Editor
A Virginia Yankee in the Civil War: The Diaries of David Hunter Strother
Chapel Hill: University of North Carolina Press, 1961, 294 pp., index

Army of Virginia
Army of the Potomac
Department of the Gulf

64

222
Fitch, Michael H.
*Echoes of the Civil War as I Hear
Them* (6th and 21st Wisconsin Infantry)
New York: R. F. Fenno & Co., 1905, 368 pp.

Army of the Ohio
Army of the Cumberland

223
Gordon, George H.
Brook Farm to Cedar Mountain (2nd
Massachusetts Infantry)
Cambridge: Riverside Press, 1883, 376 pp.

Army of Virginia
Army of the Potomac

224
Gordon, George H.
*A War Diary of Events in the War of
the Great Rebellion 1863-1865*
Boston: James R. Osgood & Co., 1882,
437 pp., index

Army of the Potomac
Department of the South
Department of the Gulf

225
Haskell, Frank A.
The Battle of Gettysburg
Madison: Wisconsin History Commission,
1908, 185 pp., index
Second Edition: Madison: Wisconsin History
Commission, 1910, 191 pp., index
New Edition: Edited by Bruce Catton,
Cambridge: Houghton Mifflin Co., 1958,
169 pp., index

Army of the Potomac

226
Hitchcock, Henry
*Marching with Sherman, Passages
from the Letters and Campaign Diaries of Henry Hitchcock*
New Haven, Connecticut: Yale University
Press, 1927, 332 pp.

Army of the Tennessee

227
Hosmer, James K.
*The Color Guard: A Corporal's Notes
of Military Service in the Nineteenth
Army Corps* (52nd Massachusetts
Infantry)
Boston: Walker, Wise & Co., 1864, 244 pp.

Department of the Gulf

228
Irving, Theodore
*"More than Conqueror" or Memori-
als of Colonel J. Howard Kitching,
Sixth New York Artillery, Army of
the Potomac*
New York: Hurd & Houghton Co., 1873,
244 pp.

229
Jackson, Oscar L.
The Colonel's Diary (63rd Ohio In-
fantry)
Sharon, Pennsylvania: Privately Printed,
1922, 262 pp.

Army of the Mississippi
Army of the Tennessee

230
Kidd, James H.
*Personal Recollections of a Cavalry-
man with Custer's Michigan Cavalry
Brigade in the Civil War* (6th Michi-
gan Cavalry)
Ionia: The Sentinel Press, 1908, 476 pp.
New Edition: Grand Rapids: The Black Let-
ter Press, 1969, 476 pp.

Army of the Potomac

231
Livermore, Thomas L.
Days and Events 1860-1866 (5th and
18th New Hampshire Infantry)
Boston: Houghton, Mifflin Co., 1920,
485 pp.

Army of the Potomac

232
Lynch, Charles H.
*The Civil War Diary of Charles H.
Lynch* (18th Connecticut Infantry)
Hartford: Privately Printed, 1915, 163 pp.

Department of West
Virginia

233
Lyon, William P.
*Reminiscences of the Civil War; Com-
piled from the War Correspondence
of Colonel William P. Lyon and from
Personal Letters and Diary by Mrs.
Adelia C. Lyon* (8th Wisconsin Infan-
try)
San Jose, California: William P. Lyon, Jr.,
1907, 277 pp.

Army of the Mississippi
Army of the Tennessee

234
Marshall, John W.
*Civil War Journal of John Wesley
Marshall, Recorded on a Daily Basis
and Sent, when Practical, to his Fi-
ance, Rachel Ann Tanner.* (97th Ohio
Infantry)
n.p., 1958, 373 pp.

Army of the Ohio
Army of the Cumberland

The Passing of the Armies

An Account of the Final Campaign of the
Army of the Potomac, Based upon
Personal Reminiscences of
the Fifth Army Corps

By

Joshua Lawrence Chamberlain

Brevet Major-General U. S. Volunteers

With Portraits and Maps

G. P. Putnam's Sons
New York and London
The Knickerbocker Press
1915

244
Williams, Edward P.
Extracts from Letters to A. B. T. from Edward P. Williams During his Service in the Civil War (100th Indiana Infantry)

New York: Privately Printed, 1903, 122 pp.

Army of the Tennessee

245
Winther, Oscar O., Editor
With Sherman to the Sea: The Civil War Letters, Diaries and Reminiscences of Theodore F. Upson (100th Indiana Infantry)

Baton Rouge: Louisiana State University Press, 1943, 181 pp.

New Edition: Bloomington: Indiana University Press, 1958, 181 pp.

Another New Edition: New York: Kraus Reprint Co., 1969, 181 pp.

Army of the Tennessee

246
Young, Jessie B.
The Battle of Gettysburg (84th Pennsylvania Infantry)

New York: Harper & Brother Publishers, 1913, 463 pp., index

New Edition: Dayton: Press of Morningside Bookshop, 1980, 452 pp., index

Army of the Potomac

Index

The numerals in this index refer to page numbers.